Spiritual Warfare

in the 21st Century:

Donald Trump
vs
The New World Order

RON MACFARLANE

Published 2018 by
Greater Mysteries Publications
Mission, BC, Canada

Cover Design: Ron MacFarlane

Printed in the United States of America

ISBN:
ISBN-13: 978-0994007797
ISBN-10: 0994007795

DEDICATION

With profound gratitude
and heartfelt admiration and respect,
this work is dedicated to Donald J. Trump
for sacrificially assuming the mantle of American president;
thereby wresting control of America's destiny
from the corrupt grip of the international establishment
and their corporate elites, in order to return democratic power
to the American people once again.

From the very start of his presidency,
Donald Trump has become the eminent defender
of religious freedom, Judeo-Christian culture and the right to
life—at home and abroad—as well as the middle-class champion
of long-term job creation, fair taxation
and equitable international trade-relations;
as well as the people's protector from Islamic terrorism,
drug smuggling, illegal immigration and
politicized intelligence agencies and court jurisdictions.

By "Making America Great Again,"
President Trump globally benefits overall world development.
"As the rose adorns itself, so does it adorn the entire garden."

May Almighty God continue to bless you with his strength,
wisdom, compassion and protection.

CONTENTS

Introduction   i

Chapter 1   The Rise of Atheistic-Socialism in Modern-Day,
             Western Society
    1.1   The Historic Roots of Socialism   1
    1.2   Christian Socialism in Victorian England   2
    1.3   The Materialistic Ideology of Marxist-socialism   3
    1.4   Subsequent Applications of Marxism   3
    1.5   The Democratic Party in America Goes Radically   4
           Left
    1.6   Identity Politics and the Democratic Party   5
    1.7   Marxist Ideology and Identity Politics   5
    1.8   Western Socialism Today is Atheistic and Anti-   6
           Christian

Chapter 2   The Cultural Revolution of the Radical-Left in
             Western Society Today
    2.1   The Countercultural Revolution of the Sixties and   9
           the "New-left"
    2.2   The Start of the "Free Love" Sexual Revolution   10
    2.3   The Mainstreaming of Homosexuality   10
    2.4   Women's Liberation and Male Emasculation   11
    2.5   White Shaming, White Guilt and White Privilege   12
    2.6   Saul Alinsky's Amoral Rules for Radical-Leftists   13
    2.7   Socialist Conformity and Compulsory Group-Think   16
    2.8   Using Micro-Aggressions to Justify Macro-   17
           Aggression
    2.9   Snowflakes, Trigger Warnings and Safe Spaces   18
    2.10   Leftist Utopia: The Victimized Oppressed become   21
           the Ruling Oppressors

Chapter 3   Globalization and the New World Order
    3.1   Empire Building in Ancient and Medieval Times   23
    3.2   World Domination through European Colonialism   25
    3.3   Nazi Germany's Twentieth-Century Attempt to Rule   26
           the World

3.4   Global Expansionism of Communist Russia during   28
and after the Second World War

3.5   World Domination through Right-Wing American   30
Hegemony and Unilateralism

3.6   George Soros and the One-World Socialist State   34

3.7   The International Financial Elite and Worldwide   37
Economic Control

3.8   Francis I: A Jesuit Pope with an International Leftist   57
Agenda

3.9   A Rational Analysis of the New World Order   65
(NWO) and One-World Government

Chapter 4   Donald J. Trump: Unlikely "Warrior of God"

4.1   Unlikely Warriors of God in Past History   89

4.2   The Prophecy of the Hermit of Loreto   97

4.3   Defending Religious Freedom, Judeo-Christian   99
Culture and Western Civilization

4.4   Necessary Qualifications to Overthrow the Elitist   105
Political and Economic Establishments

4.5   "Draining the Swamp" of Deep-State Corruption in   118
Washington, D.C.

4.6   "Making America Great Again" is not about World   129
Domination

**Chapter 5   The Underlying Spiritual Battle to Control
Mankind**

5.1   Lucifer's Age-Old Plan to Control the World   135

5.2   The Destined Incarnation of the Antichrist   137

5.3   The Forces of St. Michael and the Battle Against the   144
Dragon of Materialism

5.4   The Heavenly Kingdom of Christ-Jesus is Not of   148
This World

Conclusion   153

Appendix   157

Notes   169

Other Books   191

SPIRITUAL WARFARE

IN THE 21ST CENTURY

INTRODUCTION

A RATHER STRANGE and disturbing social upheaval has been covertly and pervasively occurring throughout the Western world—particularly in America—since the early 1990s. A creeping form of radical-socialism has been gradually infecting Western political parties, academic institutions, medical professions, mainstream news agencies, television and film industries, literary publishing and everyday social interaction for the past three decades.

Perplexingly ironic, as the former Soviet Union and Eastern Bloc States[1] were finally divesting themselves of the failed and oppressive socialist/communist ideology of the past, intellectuals and ideologues throughout the Western world began to eagerly embrace and apply the fundamental tenets of radical-socialism.

This "Westernized" form of socialist ideology is unabashedly atheistic and openly hostile to religion, particularly Christianity, in all its denominational forms. Hypocritically, however, this same "atheistic-socialism" openly supports and defends Muslim believers, who are considered members of a "victimized minority."

The philosophical underpinning of atheistic-socialism is the classic Marxist belief[2] that the social interaction of humanity throughout the ages has entirely and exclusively been a perpetual class struggle between the have-nots and the haves; the poor and the wealthy; the oppressed and the oppressors; the victims and the victimizers. In more Marxist terminology, historical class conflict has been between the "proletariat"—the peasants, labourers and workers; and the "bourgeoisie"—the nobility, landowners, and capitalists.

However, in recent times various activist groups—each one claiming "victimized" status—have adapted basic Marxist ideology to suit their own particular causes and agendas. For example, radical-feminists contend that it is men who are the real historic victimizers and that women are their primary victims. Alternatively, Black, Hispanic and Indigenous activists each claim that they are the continued victims of White, European-based culture. Homosexual activists assert that they are the victims of heterosexual, Judeo-Christian society. All these activists, therefore, blame a common oppressor for their perceived victimized condition—wealthy, White, conservative Christian men.

Moreover, in keeping with classic Marxist ideology, each of these socialist-inspired activist groups fervently believes that the solution to their perceived oppression is not gradual social change and reform; but the revolutionary overthrow of prosperous, White, Christian, male-influenced culture and society.

In essence, then, what is currently taking place throughout Western society is a fierce cultural war being waged by numerous left-leaning activist groups whose primary goal is the destruction of European-based Christian culture. In addition, their ultimate goal is to replace democratic governance through majority rule with an exclusively-atheistic, secular society where political, economic and cultural power is autocratically determined and enforced by centralized State-control that is driven by uncompromising, totalitarian-style minority activism.

In Western nations, this radical atheistic-socialism—recently termed the "alt-left"—has been opportunistically embraced by "left-wing" and "neo-liberal" political parties; but rejected by "right-wing" and "neo-conservative" political parties. Consequently, in America it is the Democratic Party (in general) that espouses and promotes alt-leftist atheistic-socialism; while the Republican Party (in general) rejects and opposes this ideology.

The radical alt-left agenda was enormously accelerated in America during the eight years (2009 to 2017) of Democratic Party President, Barack Hussein Obama. Primarily through executive order and veto power, Obama enacted and enforced radical-socialist national and international policy on climate change, economic regulation, religion, abortion, de-militarization, same-sex marriage, gun control, immigration, taxation, free-trade and deficit spending.

Moreover, through presidential appointment, Obama politicized and "weaponized" the US intelligence community (FBI, CIA and NSA), the Justice department, the IRS, the Supreme Court and district court systems with radical-socialists and alt-left loyalists. Radical-socialist ideologues within the Democratic Party and their wealthy financial backers (such as George Soros)³ were totally confident that these "deep-state" operatives in government—together with the predominantly left-leaning communications media in radio, television and newspapers—would guarantee another presidential election victory in 2017.

Moreover, Soros and his billionaire cohorts in the Democratic Alliance had decided that Hillary Rodham Clinton would be the next American president; and had set up a "dirty-tricks" Democratic Party campaign organization (headed by Soros-lackey John Podesta) to further continue and advance their accelerating alt-left cultural revolution.

Despite pre-election propaganda by major leftist-media (such as ABC, CNN, MSNBC, the NY Times and

Washington Post) that Hillary Clinton would win the presidential election by a "landslide victory"; despite the DNC (Democratic National Committee) and the Clinton election organizers conducting a corrupt, "shady-tactics" campaign in order to guarantee victory; and despite the Clinton campaign spending a record-breaking $1.2 billion to securely win the presidency—political newcomer and New York businessman, Donald J. Trump, derailed the entire alt-left revolutionary momentum by explosively winning the 2016 presidential election.

In the hours, days, weeks and months after Donald Trump's huge presidential victory (304 Electoral College votes to Clinton's 228), the alt-left—worldwide—went into complete emotional meltdown which quickly developed into a collective psychological malaise characterized by acute fear, paranoia, anxiety, depression, anger and hatred: labeled by conservative observers as "TDS—Trump Derangement Syndrome."

From Trump's powerful campaign speeches delineating his vision to "Make America Great Again (MAGA)," alt-leftist leaders and those supporting atheistic-socialism soon realized that their secular revolution was now in serious jeopardy. In the White House was everything they professed to hate—a wealthy, conservative, White, Christian male!

Moreover, Trump's vision for America was entirely contrary to atheistic-socialism: (1) instead of global homogeneity, this new president favours strong national sovereignty, legal immigration, enforced border control and a strong military; (2) instead of an entirely secularist society, this new president is intent on defending religious freedom and Judeo-Christian values and culture (such as pro-life, pro-marriage and pro-family); (3) instead of continuing to centralize authoritarian State control in Washington D.C., this new president has promised the American voter to "drain the swamp" of federal government corruption, to wrest economic power from the corporate and media elites, and to wrest political control from the self-serving Democratic and Republican establishments—thereby returning democratic power back to the American people.

Not surprisingly, then, the alt-left and their pervasive zealots in government, business, media communications, academia, psychiatry, intelligence agencies and movie industries have collectively declared war on Donald J. Trump. While radical-socialism publicly professes to promote tolerance, inclusion, diversity, political-correctness, minority rights and respect for others, the alt-left revolutionaries are hypocritically intent on destroying President Trump by whatever means available: Soros-funded riots, fake news reports, FBI surveillance, kangaroo-court challenges, drummed-up impeachment—even public outcries of assassination!

Since atheistic-socialism ideologically rejects divine moral-inspiration, divine good-counsel and divine wise-direction, it instead zealously strives to replace the ultimate moral authority of the one true God with the authoritarian and despotic control of a centralized State bureaucracy. In consequence, alt-left activist groups and political parties (either knowingly or unknowingly) play into the hands of unscrupulous billionaire globalists, such as George Soros, whose corrupt political agenda is to weaken America in order to covertly establish an elitist-controlled, one-world government—historically termed the "New World Order."[4]

President Trump, then, as the peoples' representative of "middle America" (not the leftist corporate, intellectual and media elites in New York, Washington and California) has deliberately, knowingly and sacrificially taken on the stupendous task of resisting, opposing, undoing and defeating the domestic and international forces of the New World Order.

Moreover, on an even deeper and more universal level,

since the atheistic alt-left has declared war on Christian persons, groups, beliefs, history, institutions and traditional values it is not just a cultural war that has been sweeping somnolent Western society during recent times; it is obviously a fierce spiritual battle as well. As such, the alt-left revolutionary "movement" unconsciously plays into the diabolical hands of dark spiritual beings, particularly the Antichrist, who are also intent on destroying Christianity and establishing their own evil world-domination and global-control in the near future.

Donald Trump, then, as the presidential defender of religious freedom and Judeo-Christian culture (in America and abroad) at this critical time in world history is clearly a "warrior of light," pre-destined by advanced spiritual forces to help bring America (and by extension, the rest of the world) back to the one true God of love. And while Donald Trump, as American president, clearly occupies a central role in this spiritual struggle, true victory over time will only be achieved when the vast majority of decent, honest, ethical, caring, religious, truthful and peace-loving citizens around the world rise up in unison to actively resist atheistic-socialism and the evil architects of the New World Order.

CHAPTER 1

THE RISE OF ATHEISTIC-SOCIALISM IN MODERN-DAY, WESTERN SOCIETY

1.1 The Historical Roots of Socialism

BEHAVIORILY, HUMAN BEINGS are two-fold creatures—acting either as separate individuals, or in a social context with others. Not surprisingly then, intellectual theories concerning "perfect" human society—as far back as ancient Greece—have emphasized either the "individualist" nature of human behaviour or the "socialist" nature of human behaviour.

While there has certainly been a wide variety of socialist ideas suggested throughout the centuries, socialism as an influential political movement really began around the middle of the eighteenth century as a reaction to the harsh working conditions caused by the Industrial Revolution. Various socialist models of society were proposed during this time in a sincere effort to alleviate and improve the inhumane treatment of men, women and children in mines, mills and factories.

1

Many of the early attempts at socialist reform were animated by basic Christian charity and compassion for one's fellow man. Consequently, nascent socialism regarded religion as part of the solution to poor industrial working conditions, and not part of the problem.

1.2 Christian Socialism in Victorian England

Many socialist reformers in the early-nineteenth century were devout Christians who believed that the socialist concern for the poor and the plight of the working class was quite compatible with Christian social doctrine. In fact, an entire movement in Victorian England—termed "Christian Socialism"—was founded by religious reformer, John Malcolm Ludlow (1821–1911).

Many priests and clergymen, such as Anglican Frederick Denison Maurice (1805–1872) and Broad Churchman Charles Kingsley (1819–1875) were very active within the Christian Socialist movement. Ideologically, while Christian Socialists were opposed to laissez-faire capitalism,[5] they were not interested in revolutionary change or in the radical overthrow of existing social institutions.

Christian Socialists were quite successful in establishing co-operative societies, working-men's associations, educational night-schools, a men's college (the Working Men's College in London), a women's college (Queen's College, London), journals (such as the *Christian Socialist*), profit-sharing businesses, a co-op store, and hostels in London for poor men and women.

1.3 The Materialistic Ideology of Marxist-socialism

The first seeds of anti-religious sentiment in socialist

ideology were planted during the mid-nineteenth century by "Marxist-socialism" (also referred to as "Marxist communism"). The socialist ideology of Karl Marx (1818–1883) and Friedrich Engels (1820–1895) is characterized by a completely materialistic view of human history. According to Marxism, spiritual and religious forces and factors have played absolutely no part in shaping human history. Only material, economic forces and factors are recognized. As succinctly expressed in the opening lines of *The Communist Manifesto* (1848): "The history of all hitherto existing society is the history of class struggles."

While classical Marxism wasn't ideologically anti-religious per se, since it did subscribe to a materialistic view of human history, religion was obviously dismissed as an unimportant, inconsequential and insignificant aspect of human society. Marx himself had little regard for religion, famously describing it as "the opium of the people"; that is, as a concoction of the oppressed masses intended to dull the pain and suffering of class conflict. Moreover, Marx felt it was better to abolish "the illusory happiness" of religion in favour of the "real happiness" of a classless society.

Given the low regard for religion in classical Marxism, it's rather astounding that *The Communist Manifesto* was commissioned by a secret society of religious German tradesmen—known as the League of the Just—whose goal was "the establishment of the Kingdom of God on Earth, based on the ideals of love of one's neighbor, equality and justice." In 1847, the secret society merged with a committee led by Marx and Engels to become the public "Communist League."

1.4 Subsequent Applications of Marxism

Classical Marxist-socialism, as originally formulated by Marx and Engels, spawned a number of subsequent influential branches such as: "Marxist-Leninism," "Marxist-Stalinism," "Marxist-Trotskyism" and "Marxist-Maoism." Unfortunately, these twentieth-century national applications of socialism in Russia and China were far more hostile towards established religion in their own countries, and which very often took brutal measures to abolish or suppress religious freedom.

In the democratic West, applications of Marxist-socialism were far less authoritarian and dictatorial. Historically, socialist political parties have often been disparaged and marginalized. Moreover, up until recently the primary focus of socialism in the West was on promoting and strengthening the trade union movement and on supporting political parties dedicated to workers' rights.

Nevertheless, throughout the twentieth century a number of socialist Labour Parties eventually rose to national prominence in many European countries; such as England, Ireland, Holland, Norway and Sweden; as did the Socialist Party in France, the Socialist Workers' Party in Spain, the New Democratic Party in Canada,[6] and the Labor Parties in Australia and New Zealand.

1.5 The Democratic Party in America Goes Radically Left

Up until recently, socialist political parties in America have continued to remain small, marginalized and relatively ineffectual. However, since the 1960s, more and more left-leaning activist groups began joining the Democratic Party as a means to political power.

Historically, the Democratic Party has been fundamentally social-conservative and pro-business, with minor inclusions of economic liberalism and Southern populism. While the Democratic Party has certainly entertained specific socialist policies on occasion, these have not been prevalent enough to characterized the entire Party as socialist. For example, the Democratic Party has historically promoted a welfare state together with government intervention and regulation of the economy. As well, it has traditionally supported trade unions and social programs funded by taxation.

Today, however, the Democratic Party has become completely dominated by minority activist groups, each one animated by Marxist revolutionary ideology, to the point where it is now best described as the "Democratic Socialist Party."

1.6   Identity Politics and the Democratic Party

Politically active groups based on racial, gender or cultural identity, rather than on shared principles or a common ideology, have come to be known as "identity politics." In recent years, the Democratic Party in America, and other socialist parties throughout the Western world, have become dominated by identity politics.

Rather than the traditional focus on trade unionism and working class issues, Western socialist parties are increasingly ignoring the majority of White, middle-class voters in their countries in favour of advancing the political demands of activist minority groups: such as radical feminists; homosexual and transgender activists[7]; abortion activists; secular and atheist activists; Black, Hispanic and Indigenous civil rights groups; immigration activists; and Islamic activists.

Unfortunately, by catering to well-funded and outspoken minority groups, present-day socialist parties have disenfranchised and alienated the voting majorities. Rather than democratic governance by majority rule, many Western nations have become repeatedly subjected to the legislative "tyranny of the minorities."

5

1.7 Marxist Ideology and Identity Politics

Various identity minorities have embraced and adapted classical Marxist ideology in order to rationalized their perceived oppression and to generate public sympathy. In classical Marxist doctrine, human social history is entirely and exclusively a materialistic struggle between the rich and powerful upper-class "haves"—the bourgeoisie; and the poor and powerless working-class "have-nots"—the proletariat. Happiness for the oppressed and victimized working class can only be achieved by the revolutionary overthrow of the wealthy ruling class.

In the case of radical feminists, they view all women as the victimized and oppressed class; and wealthy, White, Christian men as the historical ruling class oppressors. Similarly with homosexual and transgender activists, they view themselves as the victimized and oppressed class; and White, Christian church-goers, business-leaders and politicians as the oppressive ruling class. Various ethnic groups, such as Blacks, Hispanics, Natives and Muslims perceive themselves as oppressed social victims; and White, European-based Christian culture as the great social oppressor.

Today, throughout the Western world, each of these activist minority groups is intent on seizing political power by the revolutionary overthrow of White, European-based Christian culture—particularly wealthy, White, conservative, Christian men.

1.8 Western Socialism Today is Atheistic and Anti-Christian

Unlike the socialist ideology that sprang out of the Industrial Revolution, today's socialist ideology is radically atheistic in its zealous pursuit to establish a completely secular world-state where religion is globally marginalized and rendered politically ineffectual. Moreover, many of the activist minority groups currently view Christianity itself as one of the most serious impediments to their revolutionary usurpation of political power and control.

Consequently, what is radically occurring in today's Western society is not simply a cultural revolution, it is also spiritual warfare directed at Christian persons, groups, customs, traditions, institutions, history, values and beliefs.

CHAPTER 2

THE CULTURAL REVOLUTION OF THE RADICAL-LEFT IN WESTERN SOCIETY TODAY

2.1 The Counterculture Revolution of the Sixties and the "New-left"

THE 1960s WERE TURBULENT and tumultuous times throughout Western society. In America, social unrest was fueled largely by the Black civil rights movement, together with the anti-Vietnam War movement.

The Sixties also sparked a widespread countercultural revolution among Western youth that challenged conventional social conformity, and that openly rejected traditional conservative values and lifestyle. The countercultural revolution was also characterized by a suspicion of government authority and institutions (the "establishment"); increased concern for civil, minority and women's rights; liberation from long-established public morality (particularly concerning sexual conduct); and an acceptance of mind-altering drug experimentation and recreational use.

Consequently, the anti-conservatism of the Sixties was radically different from the traditional socialist-left, which was still primarily concerned with trade unionism and workers' rights. For this reason, the rapidly-expanding, youth-centred countercultural movement become known as the "new-left."

2.2 The Start of the "Free Love" Sexual Revolution

The public release of the birth-control pill in 1960 profoundly contributed to the sexual revolution—also referred to as the "free love" movement. The biological deception perpetrated by "the pill" was to separate sexual activity from pregnancy. If sexual activity is popularly viewed as unconnected with reproduction, then pregnancy can become callously viewed as an undesirable side-effect. Not surprisingly, then, legalized abortion (1973 in America) quickly sprang out of the sexual revolution as the solution to failed contraception.

By encouraging "free love"; that is, promiscuous extramarital sex, the sexual revolution has significantly contributed to the decline of marriage in Western society, and to the undermining of the traditional family unit. Moreover, since strong and healthy family units form the fundamental basis of a strong and vibrant society, the rapid erosion of traditional family life has caused a great deal of observable social dysfunction in Western society (such as increased drug use, inner city crime, terrorist recruitment and mental health problems).

2.3 The Mainstreaming of Homosexuality and "Permissive Society"

10

Unquestionably, for many centuries homosexuals in Western society have been the victims of cruel persecution, discrimination and harassment. And while such inhumane treatment has no place in true civil society, high moral standards of sexual conduct have historically disapproved of promiscuous sexual activity outside the protective bounds of marriage—for heterosexuals as well as homosexuals.

With the dramatic lowering of sexual moral standards that was celebrated and extolled by the "free love" sexual revolution, it was much easier for the new-left generation to accept homosexual promiscuity and non-marital sexuality—since many young heterosexuals were also engaging in similar immoral behaviour.

Even though only a small percentage of Western populations—about four percent—exhibit permanent same-sex attraction, the new-left very soon became rabidly intent on legislatively forcing everyone to believe that homosexuality was "normal," and not an anomalous condition. Moreover, a small number of noisy, well-funded and well-organized homosexual activists—together with influential leftist media—in a relatively short period of time have managed to create the illusion that homosexuality is mainstream.

By continuing to tear down the edifying moral standards of the past, the ultimate behavioral goal of the new-left soon became a revolutionary obsession to create a "permissive society" where "anything goes" between consenting adults; there would be no such thing as sexual perversion, debauchery or immorality. Today's observable result is widespread pornography, extensive child prostitution, legalized bestiality and animal brothels,[8] exhibitionist pride parades, and public sado-masochistic "kink festivals."

2.4 Women's Liberation and Male Emasculation

The women's liberation movement that began in the Sixties was very effective and influential in raising global awareness as to women's unequal access to certain jobs and professions, to the unfair wage disparity between men and women, and to male bias in language and terminology. Subsequent legal reforms in the Seventies and Eighties very successfully addressed most of these prior inequalities; such that very few women and men today identify as being "feminist."[9]

The small percentage of hard-core feminists remaining today are characteristically more militant, extremist, misandrous (male-hating) and rabidly pro-abortion. By adopting a Marxist-style ideology where all men are the oppressing victimizers in society and all women are the oppressed victims, radical-feminists similarly advocate for a revolutionary overthrow of men in society. Like all Marxist-style revolutionaries, today's radical-feminists are not striving for fairness or equality, but to usurp power for themselves over their perceived oppressors—in this case, all men.

One interesting strategy that radical-feminists have devised in their revolutionary campaign to gain absolute power over men is "internalized emasculation." By employing techniques of psychological warfare, feminist propaganda is designed to weaken men internally, rather than externally. By engaging in emotional "male shaming," instilling self-condemning "male guilt," and arousing remorseful feelings of "male privilege" radical feminists intend that a certain percentage of gullible men will voluntarily abrogate their proper role and function in society and willingly accede to being passively controlled by dominating women.

2.5 White Shaming, White Guilt and White Privilege

Various ethnic minorities that radically extol revolutionary change—such as Black, Hispanic, Aboriginal and Muslim activists—also employ techniques of psychological warfare similar to that used by radical feminists. Since these specific ethnic minorities commonly regard White, European-based Christian culture as the Marxist-style oppressor in society, they attempt to internally weaken this culture through "White shaming," and "White guilt," and accusations of unfair "White privilege."

Ethnic propaganda is intended to convince a Western nation's contemporary White majority that it is responsible for all the injustices of the past committed towards helpless minorities. Moreover, any success that White individuals obtain in today's society is denigatively regarded to be the result of White privilege, and not because of talent, honesty, hard-work, sound education or good judgement.

Furthermore, while minority groups strengthen themselves through "pride" celebrations, parades and festivals—such as Black pride, Native pride, Gay pride and Women's pride—any public celebration of White, Christian culture is vehemently denounced by the radical-left as being racist, or fascist, or neo-Nazist, or KKKist,[10] or White supremacist.

The devious leftist expectation is for the White majority—because of internalized guilt and shame for historical injustices—to voluntarily turn over the democratic reins of power to ethnic minorities. Then everyone will naively and blissfully abide in some undefined, homogenous socialist utopia.

2.6 Saul Alinsky's Amoral Rules for Radical-Leftists

Thanks primarily to the success and effectiveness of peaceful civil rights protest demonstrated by Martin Luther King Jr. (1929–1968), much of the Sixties activism undertaken by the new-left was for the most part non-violent.

These civil protests took a variety of forms; such as public marches, demonstrations, picketing, sit-ins, rallies, petition drives, teach-ins, court challenges and political lobbying..

This is not to say that there was no violence associated with the Sixties protests; only that it was more often perpetrated by intolerant law enforcement, rather than the new-left protesters. Peaceful protesters were often brutally assaulted with fire hoses, tear gas, mace, police batons, attack dogs—and on rare occasions, live ammunition.

Unfortunately, as the new-left became much more militant, extremist and radicalized over the subsequent decades, peaceful protest gradually gave way to much more violent protest. The preference of the socialist-left to engage in more violent forms of civil disobedience can be traced back to the ideological godfather of radical protest, Saul Alinsky (1909–1972).

While Alinsky's influential work: *Rules for Radicals: A Pragmatic Primer for Realistic Radicals* (1971) does not overtly promote violent protest, it is nevertheless the inescapable outcome of the fundamental ideas. For example, Alinsky does not advocate for incremental social reform, but for a radical revolution to completely overthrow the existing power structure. Moreover, he rejects any ethical or moral concerns as impediments to achieving this goal. In Alinsky's own words:

> The means-and-ends moralists, constantly obsessed with the ethics of the means used by the Have-Nots against the Haves, should search themselves as to their real political position. In fact, they are passive—but real—allies of the Haves. (*Rules for Radicals*)

In other words, for Alinsky the revolutionary end fully justifies any amoral or immoral means to achieve it (which logically would include violence).

A further inducement towards violent protest in Alinsky's

ideology is his insistence on finding and establishing an external antagonist—a "common enemy"—as a means of uniting and impelling a particular protest community. Clearly, polarizing every social protest into a warring battle between "us and the enemy" is a recipe for violence. Moreover, in a 1972 *Playboy* interview, Alinsky further elaborated on his militant outlook on life:

> All life is warfare, and it's the continuing fight against the status quo that revitalizes society, stimulates new values and gives man renewed hope of eventual progress.

Though Alinsky did not identify as a Marxist or a socialist, his radical, materialistic and revolutionary ideas are certainly similar. It's disturbing, but perhaps not surprising, to know that his ideas were openly embraced by Hillary Clinton and Barack Obama early in their careers. In Clinton's case, while attending Wellesley College in 1969, she wrote her senior thesis (with Alinsky's help) on his community organizing work. In Obama's case, during his "community organizing" period in Chicago during the 1980s, he worked for Alinsky organizations and taught seminars on Alinsky tactics and methodology of power acquisition.

Though Alinsky identified as a non-practicing Jew, his ideology clearly indicates that he was much more atheistic than religious. And though Alinsky wasn't openly anti-Christian (he had a number of Catholic supporters during life, such as Msgr. John Egan), printing a personal acknowledgement to Lucifer in his *Rules for Radicals* was clearly a deliberately-provocative, anti-Christian volley across the bow of the good ship Christianity. As written by Alinsky:

> Lest we forget at least an over-the-shoulder acknowledgment to the very first radical: from all our legends, mythology, and history (and who is to know where mythology leaves off and history begins or which is which), the first radical known to man who rebelled

against the establishment and did it so effectively that he at least won his own kingdom—Lucifer.

By glorifying the pride-filled, egotistical rebellion of Lucifer against his loving Creator—and then extolling his resultant fallen kingdom in hell—clearly demonstrates that Alinsky's radical ideology is definitely not on the side of Christianity in the spiritual warfare of our time.

2.7 Socialist Conformity and Compulsory Group-Think

Socialism, by definition, emphasizes communal and collective interaction in human society, rather than individual behaviour. The individual citizen, then, is subsumed into the whole; and is basically regarded as one replaceable cog amongst many in the overall social machine.

Not surprisingly, then, socialism typically emphasizes a kind of group or collective consciousness where everyone is expected to share the same ideology. In extreme cases, this collective ideology is legislatively enforced by the power of the state, such that citizens under a socialist government may be arrested and punished for non-compliance.

With the increased radicalization of socialist groups in the West, legislative enforcement of socialist "group-think" has become disturbingly common in recent years. In Canada, for example, the once-moderate Liberal Party has become radically leftist under the leadership of Prime Minister Justin Trudeau. Since 2013, Trudeau (in defiance of his professed Catholic faith) has tyrannically mandated that all Liberal members of parliament must now be pro-abortion.

Similarly in the US; in 2017 the new Democratic National Committee chair, Tom Perez, released a statement declaring that every Democrat in America must be pro-abortion, and that this "is not negotiable and should not change city by city or state by state." Consequently, the Democratic Party consistently votes as a unanimous bloc to continue the federal funding of nationwide abortion provider, Planned Parenthood.

What is even more disturbing and draconian with today's socialist group-think is leftist government legislation of "politically-correct" (PC) language. For example, since 4 October 2017, it is now illegal in leftist California to use the "wrong transgender pronoun." Health-care workers can now be fined up to a $1000, or jailed up to a year, for not using a transgender patient's preferred name or pronoun.

Equally disturbing in Canada, the leftist Liberals of Justin Trudeau (backed by the socialist New Democratic Party) passed legislation (M-103) on 24 March 2017 "condemning Islamophobia." Since Islamophobia is nowhere defined in the legislation, it is clearly designed to silence any free-speech criticism of Islam. No other religion was similarly singled out in the legislation for "hate speech" protection. Interestingly, since 1999 Saudi Arabia and Islamic activist groups have been unsuccessfully lobbying the United Nations for similar binding resolutions that would criminalize and silence any criticism of Islam worldwide.

2.8   Using   Micro-Aggressions   to   Justify   Macro-Aggression

Since "hate speech" has no legal definition and is therefore open to subjective opinion, today's radical-left labels anything that deviates from their ideological "group-speech" as hate speech. So for example, if someone states that they are opposed to abortion, then they are immediately accused by the radical-left of spreading hatred towards women; thereby warranting the label of "misogynist." Similarly, if someone states that they do not support same-sex marriage, then they are immediately accused by the radical-left of spreading hatred towards gays and lesbians; thereby warranting the label of "homophobe."

Recently, the radical-left has also coined an additional emotionally-charged term to describe speech that it regards as hurtful, hateful or offensive. By labeling certain words, phrases and sentences as "micro-aggressions," the radical-left is declaring that this speech is hostile, provocative and inciting.

Since micro-aggressive speech is considered to be a form of combative hostility, radical-leftist agitators feel justified in responding to this speech with "macro-aggression"; that is, with overt physical violence. One good example of this occurred on 1 February 2017, when provocative conservative speaker Milo Yiannopoulos was scheduled to talk at the University of California at Berkeley.

Leftist students were so enraged by his opposing views on political-correctness that they fomented a destructive rampage on campus to prevent him from speaking. Hundreds of protesters (some wearing black masks) hurled bricks, rocks and fireworks at the Martin Luther King Jr. Building where the sold-out speaking engagement was to occur. Some protesters used police barriers as battering rams to smash the doors of the venue; while others lit fires outside the hosting student union building, one of which engulfed a gas-powered portable floodlight.

2.9 Snowflakes, Trigger Warnings and Safe Spaces

Due primarily to the effects of extreme political-correctness, young radical-leftists (aka: "social-justice warriors or SJWs") are obsessed with the guilt-ridden possibility of saying or doing something that might possibly offend one of the many "oppressed" minorities under the socialist umbrella. Growing up in a artificial thought-cocoon where any offensive language or contrary opinion is immediately stifled or silenced has left many SJWs emotionally stunted; that is, psychologically incapable of calmly dealing with strong criticism, rational argument, opposing viewpoints or political set-back.

This was painfully evident in 2016 with the surprise election of Donald J. Trump as the 45th president of the United States. The socialist-left, worldwide, went into complete emotional meltdown: publicly screaming, yelling, swearing, rioting and crying in the streets. It was as if their entire leftist-world had come crashing down around them.

The celebrity meltdown in leftist Hollywood and the dissolute music industry was particularly shrill, hysterical, foul-mouthed, paranoid and psychotic. It was such an irrational and exaggerated response, that shocked observers began describing it as "TDS—Trump Derangement Syndrome."

Countless celebrities, such as Cher, compared the newly-elected Donald Trump to Adolf Hitler. Hollywood veteran Robert De Niro wanted to "punch Trump in the face." Actor George Clooney called President Trump a "xenophobic fascist." Oscar nominee Don Cheadle hoped that Trump would "die in a grease fire." Pop singer Miley Cyrus called Trump a "f*cking nightmare." Moreover, numerous celebrity leftists, such as Barbra Streisand, Amy Schumer, Jon Stewart, Chelsea Handler, Samuel L. Jackson and Whoopi Goldberg vowed to leave the United States if Trump got elected. None of these hypocrites did.

Perhaps the most epic celebrity meltdown was by filmmaker, actress and White-guilt-ridden, misandrous feminist Lena Dunham. In a letter published just days after Trump's Electoral College win on 8 November 2016, Dunham wrote:

> Watching the [presidential voting] numbers in Florida, I touched my face and realized I was crying. "Can we

please go home?" I said to my boyfriend. I could tell he was having trouble breathing, and I could feel my chin breaking into hives.

The meltdown continued:

At home I got in the shower and began to cry even harder. My boyfriend, who had already wept, watched me as I mumbled incoherently, clutching myself. "It wasn't supposed to go this way."

The following day, even Dunham's vagina hurt from the presidential loss, as she described it:

My voice was literally lost when I woke up, squeaky and raw, and I ached in the places that make me a woman, the places where I've been grabbed so carelessly, the places we are struggling to call our own ...

Even sadder for Dunham, she obviously didn't realize how unhinged and pathetic she sounded to anyone living in the real world. This all-too-common emotional meltdown on the left has earned SJWs the descriptor of being "snowflakes."

Currently, many young socialists have been knowingly or unknowingly indoctrinated in the "hot-house" environments of leftist universities. Instead of encouraging original thought and free-speech (as was done in the past), today's universities and colleges very often enforce mandatory, politically-correct socialist group-think and group-speech.

To shield snowflake students from dissenting opinion, politically-incorrect language or discomfiting ideas, leftist universities have begun to establish "safe spaces" on campus; which are essentially echo-chambers for radical-socialism and identity politics.

In a further effort to protect the delicate sensibilities of psychologically-coddled students, university and college lecturers are now expected to preface their speeches with "trigger warnings"; that is, cautionary forewarnings to prevent nervous listeners from hearing something offensive or disturbing; such as an unpleasant memory or the reminder of a previous traumatic experience.

While increased and sincere sensitivity to the feelings of others can be a positive development, unfortunately radical-leftist have used this sentiment as an effective rational to tyrannically limit or silence freedom of speech.

2.10 Leftist Utopia: The Victimized Oppressed become the Ruling Oppressors

Though most radical-leftists (SJWs) are busy obsessing over political-correctness, feeling victimized (or guilty) and railing against some Alinsky-inspired enemy, it's quite obvious that this worldwide coalition of disaffected minority activists does not share a clearly-defined positive social solution—other than the revolutionary overthrow of the White, conservative Christian majorities throughout the Western world.

Moreover, radical-leftists are not interested in gradual reform, obtaining equality or in sharing power. They are singularly intent on seizing total political power and state control to autocratically impose their atheistic, secular worldview on everyone in society. Historically, wherever there has been a socialist or communist overthrow of government—except for an elite handful of revolutionaries at the top of the political heap—the rest of society is dictatorially rendered powerless (including the working class). The only equality achieved in radically-socialist (communist) states is "equal misery for all"; or as stated by Winston Churchill (1874–1965):

> Socialism is a philosophy of failure, the creed of ignorance, and the gospel of envy. Its inherent virtue is the equal sharing of misery.[11]

21

In other words, the so-called leftist-minorities who currently claim to be oppressed and victimized in society aren't really interested in ending oppression and victimization at all; but in seizing political power so that *they* can become the oppressors and the victimizers instead.

Take for example the homosexual community in America. No one will deny that homosexuals haven't been cruelly oppressed and victimized in the past. But once they gained a modicum of political power under leftist administrations like that of Barak Obama, gay and lesbian activists were quick to persecute and prosecute any Christians who were opposed to their lifestyle on religious grounds. In a very short time, the oppressed gleefully became the oppressors.

Similarly with the "Me Too" movement that is currently spreading throughout Western society. While it is certainly beyond any doubt that women have historically suffered sexual victimization, assault and harassment in their jobs, professions and occupations; thankfully because of increased public awareness, protest and condemnation, many chronic victimizers have been publically exposed and held to account.

Unfortunately within the movement, there has also been a disturbing trend to vilify and condemn without due legal process. In some unjust cases, individuals have been ridiculed, scorned, censured, reprimanded, boycotted, removed and even fired—entirely on the strength of a single accusation. No investigation, no legal examination, and no court hearing. In other words, no deference to the fundamental legal principle of "innocent until proven guilty." Once again in leftist-land, the prior victims happily become the new victimizers.

CHAPTER 3

GLOBALIZATION AND THE NEW WORLD ORDER

3.1 Empire Building in Ancient and Medieval Times

UNFORTUNATELY, IT'S A SAD fact to declare that throughout human history there have been numerous megalomaniac individuals, ethnic tribes, nations and ideologies whose fanatical and deranged aspiration has been world domination—the vainglorious desire to rule and control the entire planet. Thankfully so far, all attempts have proven to be relatively short-lived and futile.

The ancient world saw a number of empires rise and fall—the Babylonian, the Assyrian and the Egyptian—entirely due to military conquest and expansion. In the sixth century BC, the Persian empire of Cyrus the Great (c.600–530 BC) stretched from Greece and northern Africa on the west, to the Indian border on the east. Two centuries later in the fourth century BC, Alexander the Great (356–323 BC) further united Greece, conquered the Persian empire and extended deeper into India; thereby establishing the largest

23

state of its time, covering about 5.2 million square kilometres. The Roman empire, however, was the most extensive social and political structure in Western civilization. At its greatest extent in the first century AD, the Roman empire completely surrounded the Mediterranean Sea; including Spain and France to the west; Britain to the north-west; the entire coast of north Africa from Mauretania to Egypt; and to Armenia and Assyria in the east.

In eastern Asia there were also huge empires militarily established in ancient times. In the third century BC, for example, Modu Chanyu (c.234–c.174 BC) founded the Xiongnu Empire in what is now Mongolia and parts of Siberia, Manchuria and Kazakhstan. Covering an area of about 9.0 million square kilometres, the Xiongnu Empire was almost twice as large as the Roman Empire.

By the thirteenth century, the Mongol Empire that was originally established by the military invasions of Genghis Khan (c.1162–1227) became the largest contiguous (connected without a break) land empire in world history. At its greatest extent, the Mongol Empire extended from Central Europe in the west to the Sea of Japan in the east; and from Siberia in the north to India and Indochina in the south. The maximum land area was about 24 million square kilometres, or about 16 % of the earth's land area.

The thirteenth century also saw the beginning of the Ottoman or Turkish Empire. At its peak in the seventeenth century, the Ottoman Empire was the same size as that of Alexander the Great—5.2 million square kilometres—that likewise included much of southeastern Europe, western Asia and northern Africa.

The rise of Muhammadism in the seventh century resulted in the military establishment of a succession of Islamic empires, known as "Caliphates," throughout the Middle East and northern Africa. The Umayyad and Abbasid Caliphates were equally extensive, comprising about 11.1 million square kilometres in area.

3.2 World Domination through European Colonialism

The Age of Discovery that began in the fifteenth century introduced a more globalized form of military conquest and domination—colonialism. During this exploratory time, many technologically-advanced European nations competitively engaged in empire building by spanning the globe and militarily acquiring satellite colonies. These colonies were typically poorly-defended and underdeveloped areas of the world that could be easily exploited for natural resources, raw materials and cheap labour in order to enrich and to strengthen the colonizing European nation.

Most notably, Spain, France, Portugal, Italy and Germany collectively established extensive domination and control over vast areas of the earth and the indigenous inhabitants that existed there. The most extensive colonial empire that was almost as large as all the other European empires combined was, of course, the British Empire. At its peak of world dominance in the late-nineteenth century, the British Empire controlled about 35.5 million square kilometres of land area; which was almost 25% or one-quarter of the earth's total available land.

During the eighteenth and nineteenth centuries, the Russian Empire—the third largest in history—reached its greatest geographical extent: 22.8 million square kilometres. Except for the large colony of Alaska in North America, the Russian Empire (like the Mongol Empire before it) contiguously stretched across Eurasia—from the Arctic Ocean in the north to the Black Sea in the south, from the Baltic Sea in the west to the Pacific Ocean in the east.

Even though a number of powerful European empires were militarily established during the Age of Colonialism, because of inter-competition and political rivalry no single empire emerged that had lasting world domination; although British superior control of the high seas by the Royal Navy did establish the British Empire as the world's first "superpower" for a brief period of time.

Throughout the twentieth century, imperialistic European empires were "de-colonized"; that is, they were geographically fractured and dismembered due to the formerly-dominated colonies gaining independent political autonomy from the previously-imperialistic European nations.

3.3 Nazi Germany's Twentieth-Century Attempt to Rule the World

Since ancient times, European tribes, ethnic territories and neighbouring nations have waged repeated warfare with each other in order to gain superior dominance and control. In the nineteenth century, for example, following the French Revolution (1789–1799), the self-appointed imperial dictator of France, Napoleon Bonaparte (1769–1821) expanded French territory in Europe through a series of brilliant military conquests. This resulted in France becoming the dominant power in much of continental Europe for a brief eleven-year period from 1804 to 1815.

Closer to the present day, there have also been horrific and evil attempts at world domination by European nations during the twentieth century; that is, by Nazi Germany and Communist Russia. In the case of Nazi Germany, when the National Socialist German Workers' Party seized ruling power under the dictatorship of Adolf Hitler (1889–1945) in 1933, one of the main goals was to undo Germany's ignominious defeat in World War I, and to restore the defeated nation to the status of a world power once again.

Since Germany had suffered critical trade shortages in WWI from Allied blockades of goods coming from colonies overseas, Nazi Germany was determined to prevent any future recurrence by militarily expanding its territorial outreach within Europe itself. Territorial expansion as a nationalistic "right" in order to strengthen and protect Nazi Germany (the "Third Reich") was rationalized into a governing policy known as "Lebensraum." The first Nazi application of Lebensraum was the military invasion of Poland in 1939. As a result of this hostile incursion, Britain and France declared war on Germany; thereby igniting World War II.

Nazi German military expansionism and the drive for world domination were also rationalized by the fanatical doctrine that German people (the "Aryan races") were racially superior to all others. Nazi leaders declared, therefore, that Germany had a moral right and nationalistic duty to conquer and subjugate the world's inferior races. In what would become a horrific evil stain on human history, the Nazi cult of racial superiority genocidally murdered about six million European Jews; and savagely targeted another 5.5 million "enemies of the German state": homosexuals, handicapped persons, communists, Slavs and Romani (Gypsies).

As a result of Nazi wartime imperialism, by 1944 Germany dominated the entire European continent, which included: Poland, Finland, Romania, Denmark, Norway, Luxembourg, the Netherlands, Belgium, France, Greece, Albania, Estonia, Latvia, Lithuania, Yugoslavia, Belorussia, most of the Ukraine, large tracts of Russian territory (including Leningrad in the north and Rostov in the south), northern and central Italy, Hungary and Slovakia—and additionally controlled Libya and Egypt in north Africa.

During World War II, Nazi Germany joined forces with Fascist Italy under dictator Benito Mussolini (1883–1945), and Imperial Japan under Emperor Hirohito. Prior to

27

collaborating with Nazi Germany, Imperial Japan already had plans of its own for territorial expansion and domination. By 1931, Japan had invaded and conquered Manchuria (Northeast China); and in 1937, it invaded China proper thereby occupying Nanking and Beijing. Later in 1938, Japan unsuccessfully attempted to claim Soviet Union territory bordering on occupied Manchuria.

To further its long-term expansionist plan of establishing a Japanese Empire throughout Southeast Asia, in 1941 Imperial Japan devastatingly launched simultaneous military attacks against the United States (specifically the Pacific Fleet at Pearl Harbour), Hong Kong, British Malaya and the Philippines. At the peak of its wartime expansion in 1942, Japan also controlled Borneo, Central Java, Cepu, Dutch New Guinea, Malang and Sumatra; as well as several key islands in the Pacific (including Guadalcanal).

Thankfully by 1945, the Allied nations (including China and the USSR) had successfully defeated the evil, world-domination plans of Nazi Germany, Fascist Italy and Imperial Japan. Tragically, this defeat involved 30 countries around the world, and resulted in the deaths of 50 to 85 million people, most of whom were innocent civilians.

3.4 Global Expansionism of Communist Russia during and after the Second World War

Prior to 1941 when Nazi troops invaded Russian territory, the Soviet Union, under the dictatorship of Joseph Stalin (1878–1953), was aligned with Germany. During this time, in concert with Nazi Germany, the Soviet Union militarily annexed several European countries: Lithuania, Estonia, Latvia, Moldavia and Karelia (eastern part of Finland)—immediately restructuring them into communist republics within the USSR (Union of Soviet Socialist

Republics). Moreover, immediately following the end of the war, the Soviet Union continued to occupy several other European countries that had been liberated by Russian troops: Poland, Romania, Czechoslovakia, Hungary, Yugoslavia, Bulgaria, Albania and East Germany.

The Central and Eastern European countries that the Soviet Union continued to dominate and control as communist "puppet states" came to be known as the Eastern Bloc. To the Soviet Union, the Eastern Bloc served as a protective shield against any future European invasion. To Western democracies, however, these imperialistically-acquired satellite countries were regarded as disturbing and alarmist examples of Communist Russian expansionism. In 1947, the United States enacted the Truman Doctrine, a foreign policy designed to assist any nation threatened by Soviet expansion. Additionally, in 1949 nine Western European countries as well as Britain, the United States and Canada formed a military alliance known as "NATO": the North Atlantic Treaty Organization to counter further Soviet imperialistic aggression.

In the years following the end of World War II, the United States and the Soviet Union emerged as the world's two great "superpowers." Unfortunately, since the US was a republican democracy and the USSR was a communist dictatorship, inevitable political and military tension was soon to erupt. Moreover, with military and financial assistance from the Soviet Union, communism spread rapidly throughout the entire world in the post-war years.

Since both superpowers possessed nuclear weapons by 1949, each country was fearfully reluctant to engage in direst warfare with the other. As Soviet expansionism continued, local clashes between US democracy and Russian communism were fought by proxy groups, governments and militias—one side backed and supported by the United States, and the other side backed and supported by the Soviet Union.

29

This small-scale, recurrent and localized military engagement throughout the modern world came to be known as the "Cold War."

By the time the USSR officially collapsed in 1991, Russian-backed communism had spread throughout the world; to Cuba, Grenada, Benin, the Congo, Angola, Mozambique, Ethiopia, Somalia, Yemen, Afghanistan, Mongolia, Korea, Vietnam, Laos and Kampuchea.

3.5 World Domination through Right-Wing American Hegemony and Unilateralism

Throughout the Cold War years, the United States was not merely countering Russian communist expansionism by conventional military engagement in proxy wars; but was also expanding its own global sphere of dominance by increasing its nuclear arsenal, by undertaking extensive propaganda campaigns, by employing psychological warfare, and by establishing worldwide counterintelligence and espionage networks. Moreover, the collapse of the USSR in 1991 left the United States as the only remaining superpower.

With the demise of the Soviet Union as a rival superpower, one would have expected that consequent American foreign policy would be to significantly reduce military spending, and to curtail strategic military positioning abroad. Not surprisingly, however, certain right-wing ideologues and powerful government officials in the US saw the end of the Cold War as an auspicious opportunity to establish complete American world-dominance through superior economic and military might.

Noteworthy among those in the first post-Cold War administration of President George H. W. Bush who were adamantly opposed to military budget cuts and overseas troop reductions were Dick Cheney (then Secretary of

Defense), General Colin Powell (then Chairman of the Joint Chiefs of Staff), and Paul Wolfowitz (then Undersecretary of Defense for Policy). Moreover, all three individuals were responsible for drafting a series of Defense Strategy documents that outlined a plan for unrivaled American dominance in world affairs ("hegemony") through nuclear capability, military superiority and economic control. Colin Powell bluntly shared the "Cheney Plan" in 1992 before the House Armed Services Committee by stating:

> I want [the American military] to be the bully on the block ... there is no future in trying to challenge the armed forces of the United States.

Furthermore, as the only existing superpower, the United States would be capable of acting unilaterally to ensure its national interests and to maintain world order; that is, to enforce a global "Pax Americana."

Unfortunately for Cheney, Powell and Wolfowitz, though the United States was able to flex its military muscle in the 1990-1991 Gulf War against Iraqi dictator Saddam Hussein (1937–2006), a large federal budget deficit, an economic recession, and the 1992 presidential defeat of George H. W. Bush to Democrat Bill Clinton put the brakes on their plan for absolute American hegemony.

In spite of this temporary set-back, Cheney, Powell and Wolfowitz—outside of political office—continued to harbour and fine-tune their plan for world domination. In 1997, a right-wing think tank was created in Washington, DC called the Project for the New American Century (PNAC). In September 2000, the PNAC published a 90-page report entitled "Rebuilding America's Defenses: Strategies, Forces, and Resources for a New Century." The report was essentially a blueprint strategy for American hegemony. Not surprisingly, Dick Cheney and Paul Wolfowitz were signatories to the PNAC "Statement of Principles." Also worth noting were the endorsement signatures of Jeb Bush (then Governor of Florida) and Donald Rumsfeld (the Secretary of Defense under Gerald Ford).

In 1998, when George W. Bush decided to run for president, Cheney and his fellow hegemonists saw a second golden opportunity to re-enact their dream of world domination and control. Since George Bush Jr. had little knowledge of US foreign policy, George Bush Sr. put together a campaign advisory team headed by Condoleezza Rice (National Security Council Advisor to Bush Sr.) called the "Vulcans." Other key members of the team included Paul Wolfowitz, Scooter Libby (Deputy Under-Secretary of Defense for Policy under Bush Sr.) and Richard Perle (Assistant Secretary of Defense for Strategic Affairs under Reagan). Though not members, close associates of the Vulcan group included Dick Cheney, Colin Powell and George Shultz (US Secretary of State under Reagan).

Predictably, all members and associates of the Vulcans received key administrative positions when George W. Bush defeated Democratic Vice-President Al Gore in 2001 to become the 43rd President of the United States—as indicated by the following:

- Condoleezza Rice was appointed US National Security Advisor and later US Secretary of State in Bush's Second Administration.
- Paul Wolfowitz was appointed US Deputy Secretary of Defense under Donald Rumsfeld and later president of the World Bank in 2005.
- Richard Perle was appointed chairman of the US Defense Policy Board Advisory Committee.
- Scooter Libby became Chief of Staff to the Vice President of the United States.
- Dick Cheney was appointed Vice-President of the United States.
- Colin Powell became United States Secretary of State

- George Shultz served as an informal advisor to the President.

One thing Cheney and company concluded from their expansionist efforts under George Bush Sr. was that without some disastrous world event, establishing world domination would likely be a long and tedious process. This acquiescence was delineated in the PNAC report, "Rebuilding America's Defenses" (2000) as follows:

> Further, the process of [US hegemonic] transformation, even if it brings revolutionary change, is likely to be a long one, absent some catastrophic and catalyzing event—like a new Pearl Harbor.

Lo and behold, one amazingly-fortuitous, catastrophic event just "happened" to occur on 11 September 2001—the terrorist attacks on the World Trade Centre in New York, and on the Pentagon Building in Virginia. Cheney, Rumsfeld, Wolfowitz, Perle and company immediately put their world domination plan into action—in the guise of a "War on Terrorism"—by invading Afghanistan in 2001 and then Iraq in 2003. While a flimsy case can be made to invade Afghanistan immediately after the terrorist attacks since the principal perpetrator, Osama bin Laden (1957–2011), was reportedly hiding out there, invading Iraq two years later on a similar pretext was deceitful and fraudulent since most of the 19 hijackers were citizens of Saudi Arabia, and since Iraq posed no terrorist threat.

When in January 2002, President George W. Bush referred to the "Axis of Evil" as being Iraq, Iran and North Korea, it quickly became obvious after the Iraq invasion that these were the first three military targets on the road to world domination. In May 2002, then-Undersecretary of State John Bolton hinted that follow-up, preemptive military strikes—"Beyond the Axis of Evil"—would be Cuba, Libya and Syria.

Unfortunately for Cheney, Rumsfeld and their fellow imperialists, the US military got hopelessly bogged down in Afghanistan and in Iraq. The massive aerial assault on Bagdad that began the military invasion in 2003 was intended by Defense Secretary Rumsfeld to be an effective campaign of "Shock and Awe"; that is, a spectacular display of overwhelming military force and superior intelligence intended to paralyze the Iraqi enemy and their will to fight. Unfortunately, what it did instead was to galvanize determined Iraqi resistance, and to arouse unified worldwide condemnation.

Cheney, Rumsfeld and the other Bush-imperialists naively believed that invading Iraq would be easy; and that once the country and its oil fields were secured, it would provide a strategic foothold in the Middle East from which to launch further invasions into Iran and Syria. But once again, their sordid dream for American world domination failed miserably; and proved instead to be nothing but an egomaniacal, delusional nightmare—especially for hundreds of thousands of innocent civilian casualties in Iraq and Afghanistan.

3.6 George Soros[12] and the One-World Socialist State

Together with the 2008 financial crisis (the "Great Recession") and Hurricane Katrina in 2005, the Iraq War fiasco was a huge contributing factor in George W. Bush's widespread unpopularity in his second term of office. Consequently, the Democratic Party regained control of Congress in the 2006 elections, and a Black Democratic Party candidate—Barak Hussein Obama—was elected as the 44th US President in 2008.[13]

Beginning in 2009, therefore, with the election of a Democratic Party president, together with Democratic Party control of the House and the Senate, American politics, finances and culture took a pendulum swing to the hard left. Moreover, in the same way that George W. Bush was an unsuspecting front-man for right-wing American imperialists, Barak Obama was the unsuspecting front-man for leftist billionaires and one-world globalists—particularly the egomaniacal George Soros.[14]

Aside from their irrational lust for world domination, sinister globalists such as George Soros noticeably differ from right-wing imperialists as to exactly how to achieve it. For example, ruling the world through American imperialism requires an ultra-strong America, nationalistically and militarily; whereas ruling the world with a one-world socialist government requires all nations—including America—to relinquish their national sovereignty and to forfeit their individual militaries.

George Soros, therefore, does everything he can to weaken the United States; a strong America is a serious impediment to his sordid globalist intentions. As he himself has publicly stated: his intention is to burst the "bubble of American supremacy" because US preeminence in the world is a detriment to global "equilibrium"; that is, "one-world socialism."

One Soros-inspired strategy to weaken American sovereignty—used throughout the Obama presidency—is to encourage and support illegal immigration into the United States, and to flood the country with unvetted Muslim "refugees." Not only does this cause confusion in the social and cultural fabric of the nation; but it also puts tremendous strain on the nation's economy in order to governmentally support this immigration tsunami. Predictably, Soros and his fellow globalists have also been instrumental in the "migrant crisis" sweeping many present-day European nations.

Despite the accolades and hero-worship bestowed by the financial sharks in the investment world, socialist billionaires (aka: "limousine leftists) like George Soros are the bottom-feeders of the real economy. They reap their enormous wealth entirely by currency manipulation. Their riches aren't derived from creating, inventing, manufacturing and/or selling value-added goods and services; they don't produce anything of social benefit—they just make money by manipulating money.

The puzzling question naturally arises, however, since these leftist billionaires acquired their inordinate wealth from free-market capitalism, why do they want to establish a world-wide socialist state? The answer is obvious from the failed example of every socialist and communist state that has ever been tried—the uber-rich and powerful use the socialist system to maintain their exceptionally-wealthy status as a circumscribed and centralized all-controlling elite. The remainder of the population, unfortunately, are forced to be financially flat-lined and rendered powerless by the abolition of private property and through "income equality"—the forced redistribution of all private wealth (except that of the controlling elite, of course).

As the darling of the radical-left, George Soros is often praised for his generous philanthropy, and credited with effecting positive social change in the US and abroad. Soros' "philanthropy," however, is better described as covert subversion through "dark money"; [15] and his "social change" is better described as geopolitical interference[16] and leftist social engineering.

The problem with today's multi-billionaires like George Soros is that their personal wealth is greater than the GDP[17] (national worth) of many countries in the world. The disturbing result is that the uber-rich very often behave like unelected politicians or government officials. In Soros' case, his geopolitical interference is more like a borderless rogue nation: fomenting regime change, instigating revolutions, funding political uprisings and toppling national currencies.[18]

Similarly echoed by Chrystia Freeland, Global Editor of *Reuters*: "Today's super-rich are increasingly a nation unto themselves."

If Soros' philanthropic activities are truly positive and "progressive,"[19] why are they all covertly funded by dark money? Disturbingly, Soros has assembled a complex and pervasive global network of leftist non-profit organizations,[20] most of which are centrally funded by Open Society Foundations (OSF)—a private, multi-billion dollar, tax-exempt organization founded by Soros in 1993. With branches in 37 countries, the OSF is a multi-headed hydra of worldwide leftist agitation—such as the international promotion of abortion, open borders, Muslim migration and the homosexual lifestyle.

Recently in 2017, to help ensure that his radical-left global activism and interventionism continues after his death, the now 88-year-old Soros pumped $18 billion of his ill-gotten fortune into Open Society Foundations. Since the rapidly-aging Soros is unlikely to realize his goal of a one-world socialist government in this life (thanks to increased public awareness of his nefarious machinations and to the presidential election of Donald Trump) presumably his "mini-me" son Alexander (age 32) and his older brother Jonathan (age 47) will continue the family dream of world domination into the future.

3.7 The International Financial Elite and Worldwide Economic Control

3.7.1 The Development of Banking in Ancient Times

While there continue to be right-wing and left-wing political forces in existence today that covertly strive for worldwide political domination and international government control, there are also non-political forces that have been historically at work to gain complete power and control of the global economy and money supply. The rationale behind this particular pathological pursuit of power is the notion that if you control the world's monetary supply, then you effective control the various nations of the world. Similarly expressed as a fundamental maxim attributed to the super-wealthy House of Rothschild: "Let us control the money of a country and we care not who makes its laws."

For as long as human beings have gathered, retained and shared certain articles and items of considered value—such as grain, cattle, jewelry, artwork, precious metals, natural rarities, luxury materials and currency—there has been a need to store, house, protect, save, trade, lend and borrow these things. That is, there has been a need for treasuries, coffers, repositories, store facilities, counting houses, vaults, exchanges, stockpiles, warehouses and reserves; in other words—banks.

Historically as well, as long as there has been rulers, monarchs, kings, queens, pharaohs, czars, mandarins, emperors, empresses, potentates, caliphs, chieftains, sovereigns, shahs, sultans, caesars, kaisers, khans, maharajas, moguls and overlords—there has been a totalitarian desire and a practical need to centralize the royal banking systems.

Centralizing the accumulation of wealth naturally conferred immense power and control for the autocratic rulers involved. But in a less egocentric way, however, centralization also provided a stabilizing regulation and uniformity to the trade, commerce and business activity of the ordinary mass of people. The exchange of goods and services is rendered much easier with a universally-recognized (or imposed) and widely-usable system.

Throughout ancient times, then, the various centralized banking systems and the interconnected issuance of currency were under the monopolistic power and control of the autocratic rulers. As indicated biblically when Christ-Jesus asked the Pharisees:

"Show me the money for the tax." And they brought him a coin. And Jesus said to them, "Whose likeness and inscription is this?" They said, "Caesar's." Then he said to them, "Render therefore to Caesar the things that are Caesar's." (Matt 22:19–21)

During this time, macroeconomic centralized banking was certainly not in the controlling grip of private, non-aristocratic hands. On a microeconomic level, however, some ordinary market transactions—such as exchanging currency, tax collecting, borrowing and lending—were legally conducted by private citizens. Once again as described biblically in Matthew (21:12):

And Jesus entered the temple of God and drove out all who sold and bought in the temple, and he overturned the tables of the money-changers and the seats of those who sold pigeons.

In ancient times these small-scale, privately-conducted monetary transactions were usually done in the streets or around temple buildings using small, portable tables or benches. Hence the English word "bank" derives from the Italian "banca" meaning bench or countertop. Not surprisingly, since the Greek and Roman empires loosely amalgamated numerous city-states and ethnic territories—each having their own currencies—there was a ubiquitous need to convert foreign money into the authorized coinage of the empire.

3.7.2   Banking and Currency During the Middle Ages

The gradual dissolution of the Roman Empire gave rise to several separate European kingdoms and monarchies; such as the Kingdom of Hungary, the Kingdom of Bulgaria, the Kingdom of Serbia, the Kingdom of Bohemia, the Kingdom of Poland, the Kingdom of France, the Kingdom of Italy, the Kingdom of Burgundy, the Kingdom of Aragon and the Kingdom of England. Although the various kingdoms would often create their own coinage (such as the ducatus, the florin, the dobla, the gros, the farthing and the groat), much of the day-to-day trading that occurred during the Middle Ages was done by "bartering"; that is by swapping actual goods and services at the moment of exchange (without using a medium of trade, such as money).

Although there was some standardization of currency exchange throughout Western and Central Europe during the ninth-century reign of Holy Roman Emperor, Charlemagne (742–814), it was really during the Holy Land Crusades in the twelfth and thirteenth centuries that international banking really began to develop—thanks to the Knights Templar.

3.7.3 The Development of International Banking and the Knights Templar

The Knights Templar was a Catholic military order of "warrior monks" that was founded in 1119 for the express purpose of protecting European pilgrims journeying to Jerusalem and the Holy Land. Not only were pilgrims in danger of being attacked and robbed en route; but the greatest threat was from Muslim fanatics who were intent on massacring Christian "infidels" as their Islamic "duty."

As a secure path of protection from Europe to the Holy Land, the Templars established a well-connected chain of castles, monasteries and fortifications that could safely store, record-keep and transfer money and valuables for travelling pilgrims—in effect, the first international safety deposit system. The Templars also began to issue "notes" to pilgrims for money deposited at one location that could be used to reclaim money at a distant location. In other words, the Templars pioneered the use of travelers' cheques as well.

Furthermore, the financial protection by warrior knights was so secure that European royalty and nobility soon began securing their own valuables within the Templar monasteries; which quickly developed into an international system of "banking houses" for the Order. As a result, the Templar banking operations were so universally popular and widely used that only 10% of the Order became warrior knights; the remaining 90% became "banking monks."

Since many prominent Templars were from wealthy French and English families, the Order financially benefited from valuable endowments of land, castles and money. Moreover, since individual Knights were obligated to take a strict vow of poverty, they would often bequeath their own personal wealth to the Order. Moreover, the Church permitted the Templar Order to keep any riches confiscated from Muslims in the course of battle.

Not surprisingly then, the Templar Order (not the individual knights) became extremely wealthy in assets, with a central treasury located in Paris. The Templars soon acquired their own Mediterranean fleet of ships to transport knights, pilgrims, goods, supplies, valuables and armaments back and forth from Europe to the Holy Land. With their accumulated wealth, the Templar "bankers" were also able to issue and document large-scale loans to various royal houses to help finance their nationwide political activities.

Tragically, the Templar policy of making large-scale loans to royalty resulted in the Order's brutal demise. Since Phillip IV (1268–1314), the iniquitous king of France, was deeply in debt to the Templars to finance his war with the English, rather than repay his debt he decided to destroy the Order and seize its wealth in Paris instead.

According to legend, when the Templar Grand Master Jacques de Molay and the Templar Preceptor of Normandy

Geoffrey de Charney were burned at the stake in 1314, de Molay predicted out of the flames that both King Phillip and his puppet Pope Clement V (c.1264–1314) would meet him before the judgement seat of God in less than a year. Clement died a month later, and Phillip died in a hunting accident before the year ran out.

While the Knights Templar are legendary in history for their Christian devotion, their military gallantry and their treacherously-orchestrated demise, they should also be better recognized and appreciated as the pioneers of modern international banking. It is important to remember as well that the international banking organization established by the Knights Templar was entirely non-profit and conducted by a Catholic Order (and not by private citizens). No individual knight financially benefited from the monetary transactions of the Order. In fact, individually-wealthy knights sacrificed their own personal fortunes by faithfully adhering to the Templar's obligatory vow of poverty.

3.7.4 The House of Rothschild and Privately-Controlled International Banking

The first, high-finance international banking organization that was successfully owned and operated by private citizens was established in the eighteenth century as the Banking House of Rothschild. The Rothschild banking empire had humble beginnings with Mayer Rothschild (1744–1812) who was raised in a Jewish ghetto in Frankfurt. He learned commodities trading in rare coins, silk and other goods—as well as currency trading—primarily from his father. One of the family's high-profile clients was Prince Wilhelm of Hesse-Kassel (1787–1867), who later made Mayer the financial agent for the Crown in 1769.

Beginning in 1789, Mayer's trading and financial lending services were enormously enriched by the ten-year upheaval of the French Revolution. During this time, Rothschild supplied the Austrian army with uniforms, horses, military equipment and food (such as wheat). He also arranged for regular monetary payments to Hessian mercenary soldiers.

The expanding Rothschild banking services in Frankfurt became truly international when Mayer sent out four of his five sons to establish family-held banking houses in other important European capital cities: London, Paris, Naples and Vienna. The eldest son, Amschel (1773–1855), acceded as head of the bank in Frankfurt after his father's death. Together with the regular channels of correspondence (such as private messenger and mail delivery), each of the five banking houses was cleverly kept in close communication through a sophisticated network of carrier pigeons.

The newly-established Rothschild international banking system reaped huge but questionable financial rewards from its cross-border involvement in the Napoleonic Wars between 1803 to 1815. Nathan Rothschild (1777–1838) in London, for example, by loaning the British government funds to pay its troops, by organizing the shipment of gold bullion to British armies across Europe, and by managing and financing various government subsidies to Britain's allies, almost single-handedly financed the British war effort against Napoleon Bonaparte (1769–1821).

Nevertheless, in spite of his enormous financial assistance to Britain during this time, Nathan was also secretly funding Napoleon as well. Moreover, even though Rothschild knew in advance of the English public that Britain had won the Battle of Waterloo, he began selling off all his bonds as if Napoleon had won, which would effectively render British currency worthless. His actions caused a panicked public sell-off which totally collapsed the English stock exchange. Rothschild's agents then swooped in like vultures and gobbled up the discarded stocks and bonds at rock-bottom prices. By the time the English public was informed of Wellington's victory,

Nathan Rothschild had surreptitiously seized control of the English stock exchange.

It should also be noted that while the Rothschild bank in London was helping fund British wars and colonial expansion, the Rothschild bank in Paris—"De Rothschild Frères"—established by James Rothschild (1792–1868) was simultaneously helping fund French wars and colonial expansion. It was in fact the De Rothschild Frères bank that funded Napoleon's brief return from Elba after he had been banished there by Britain and the Allied Powers.

Even though the Rothschild international banking empire has historically contributed in numerous positive ways to the growth and development of Western society around the world—financing infrastructure projects such as railways and the Suez Canal, rescuing national banks, furnishing credit to various governments during times of crisis, and contributing philanthropically to countless charities, it is the instances of market manipulation, war profiteering and the amoral funding of both national combatants in an armed conflict that have primarily fueled historical suspicion of Rothschild financial ethics and monetary intentions.

Moreover, the fact that Rothschild international banking investments have historically been so globally pervasive, reaching into all areas of Western society; such as: financing the De Beers diamond monopoly; funding British imperialist Cecil Rhodes (1853–1902), along with the creation of the Rhodes Scholarship and the African colony of Rhodesia; financially assisting Brazil to become independent from Portugal; being involved from 1919 to 2004 in fixing the London price of gold; and being one of the controller families of the East India Company—has greatly contributed to the copious conspiratorial theories which claim that the Rothschild family dynasty has been covertly controlling world events for the past two centuries.

Add to this the preeminent secrecy of the Rothschild

family fortune, the tight-lipped inter-family relationships, the private ownership of their numerous banks and businesses, and their characteristic avoidance of overt publicity and unwelcomed attention—and you have even more conspiratorial reasons to suspect that the Rothschild dynasty is unduly controlling the destiny of nations.

A more level-headed assessment, however, recognizes that much of the Rothschild family fortune was amassed during a time when monarchies ruled European nations, and currencies were backed by gold reserves. When crown-royalties had insufficient gold to fund expensive national ventures (such as war), then they were forced to borrow the gold-backed currency that they needed—hence the financial dependency on the Rothschild international banking system.

Today European nations are run by democratic governments with regulated central banks that can print their own necessary currency without any gold backing—hence the lack of any modern dependency on the Rothschild bullion banks. Despite the recurring fears of conspiracy theorists, with the current complex inter-governmental control of international banking it is quite impossible for the Rothschild family dynasty to exclusively control the world economy. Nor is it likely that any of today's numerous Rothschilds are even remotely interested in the logistical nightmare of world domination. It is much more likely that family members are more concerned with simply maintaining their inherited wealth in an unpredictably-volatile world market, than in pursuing some futile global despotic dream.

3.7.5 Western Democracies and the Establishment of Government-Controlled Central Banks

As rulerships and monarchies discovered in ancient times, establishing centralized control of a nation's banking transactions had many positive trading benefits. For one, it provided some long-term stability to future economic uncertainty. Moreover, standardizing a nation's currency of exchange made it much easier to conduct small-scale, everyday business transactions throughout a nation's economy. Centralized banking also helped to control the money supply and the quality of the currency being used in a nation's economy.

During the late-nineteenth and early-twentieth centuries, as Western nations gradually discarded the yoke of monarchial rulership in favour of democratically-elected governance, centralized banking and currency issuance were logically placed under government control rather than surrendered into the profiteering hands of privatized control.

The Bank of England is considered the model on which most modern central banks have been derived. Though it was originally established in 1694, it was not until the Bank Charter Act of 1844 that the Bank of England had sole control over the issuance of new bank notes; and not until the 1870s that it reluctantly became the "lender of last resort" to other banks in financial crisis.

Surprisingly, the Bank was privately owned by stockholders right up until 1946 when it was eventually nationalized by the British government. Moreover, since 1998, though it is legislatively owned by the Treasury Solicitor on behalf of the government, the Bank of England functions as an independent public organization with autonomous authority in setting monetary policy.

Likewise is the US Federal Reserve ("the Fed"), the central banking system of the United States that was next established in 1913. Although the Federal Reserve is an instrument of the US government, according to its own statement it is:

> an independent central bank because its monetary policy decisions do not have to be approved by the President or anyone else in the executive or legislative branches of government, it does not receive funding appropriated by

the Congress, and the terms of the members of the Board of Governors span multiple presidential and congressional terms.

Subsequent to the establishment of the US Federal Reserve, other countries soon followed suit with central banks of their own: Australia in 1920, Peru in 1922, Colombia in 1923, Mexico and Chile in 1925; and Canada,[21] India and New Zealand in 1934.

3.7.6 Are Central Banks Secretly Controlling the World Economy?

Public and political suspicion and alarm concerning the secretive and self-serving misbehaviour of certain wealthy financiers and high-finance banking institutions throughout modern history[22] has also fuelled countless conspiracy theories about an international financial elite that is (or intends on) controlling the world economy. No doubt the duplicitous funding of European warfare by the House of Rothschild has significantly contributed to this widespread distrust and apprehension. One similar noteworthy concern was expressed by Thomas Jefferson (1743–1826) in a letter to John Taylor, dated 28 May 1816 :

> And I sincerely believe, with you, that banking establishments are more dangerous than standing armies; and that the principle of spending money to be paid by posterity, under the name of funding, is but swindling futurity on a large scale.

A more recent alarmist warning was sounded in a 1922 speech by New York Mayor John F. Hylan (1868–1936):

> The real menace of our Republic is the invisible government, which like a giant octopus sprawls its slimy legs over our cities, states and nation. To depart from

mere generalizations, let me say that at the head of this octopus are the Rockefeller-Standard Oil interests and a small group of powerful banking houses generally referred to as the international bankers. The little coterie of powerful international bankers virtually run the United States government for their own selfish purposes ...

These international bankers created the central banks of the world (including the Federal Reserve), and they use those central banks to get the governments of the world ensnared in endless cycles of debt from which there is no escape. Government debt is a way to "legitimately" take money from all of us, transfer it to the government, and then transfer it into the pockets of the ultra-wealthy.

What appears to be the strongest reason to think that the world economy is controlled by a secretive financial elite is the misconception that central banks—particularly the US Federal Reserve—are privately owned and operated; that is, they are covertly controlled by some undefined wealthy cabal. While it is certainly true that some central banks were privately owned by shareholders when they were originally established (such as the Bank of England and the Bank of Canada), this is no longer the case.

Similar to the judicial systems in today's democracies, it is wisely necessary for central banking systems to also have a healthy measure of independence from governmental decision-making in order to avoid undue political interference and partisanship. Even so, central banks have been established by federal legislation and are ultimately answerable to democratic government regulation and oversight—not some wealthy elite.

3.7.7 What about the Multinational Bank for International Settlements—Does it Control the World Economy?

The little-known fact that there is a multinational central

bank in Basel, Switzerland, that is comprised of numerous national central banks—known as the Bank for International Settlements (BIS)—has also given rise to recent concerns of possible secretive control of the world economy.

Certainly fueling conspiracy theorists is the BIS's rather nefarious past. The BIS was originally established in 1930 by the U.S., Britain, France, Germany, Belgium, Italy, Switzerland and Japan primarily in order to handle German reparation payments following World War I. Soon afterward, when World War II broke out in 1939, although the BIS was to officially remain relatively inactive and neutral, it was later found to be conducting banking operations helpful to Nazi Germany, such as laundering their looted gold.[23]

Not surprisingly, then, at the end of the War the Allies decided to dissolve the BIC; although this decision was later reversed. Beginning in 1950, the BIS assisted the post-war European countries in restoring currency convertibility and free, multilateral trade.

The gradual development of the BIS as the "central bank for central banks" was not by accidental design; but was clearly one of its core purposes from the beginning, as explicitly stated in the original founding documents of 1930:

> The objects of the Bank are: to promote the co-operation of central banks and to provide additional facilities for international operations; and to act as trustees or agent in regard to international financial settlements entrusted to it under agreements with the parties concerned.

This original statement has been subsequently clarified, and the current threefold mission of the BIS is presently stated to be:

> to serve central banks in their pursuit of monetary and financial stability, to foster international cooperation in these areas, and to act as a bank for central banks.

For those conspiracy theorists who are already suspicious and fearful of national central banks, the very existence of a multinational central bank—the Bank for International Settlements—is regarded as definitive proof that the world economy is controlled by a financial elite. This notion has been succinctly expressed by Georgetown University history professor Carroll Quigley (1910–1977) in *Tragedy and Hope: A History of the World in Our Time* (1966):

> The powers of financial capitalism had another far-reaching aim, nothing less than to create a world system of financial control in private hands able to dominate the political system of each country and the economy of the world as a whole. This system was to be controlled in a feudalist fashion by the central banks of the world acting in concert, by secret agreements arrived at in frequent private meetings and conferences. The apex of the system was to be the Bank for International Settlements in Basel, Switzerland, a private bank owned and controlled by the world's central banks which were themselves private corporations.

While it is eminently plausible that there are in existence disreputable and power-hungry globalist financiers who would dearly love to control the world economy through the Bank for International Settlements; fortunately, as the organization is presently constituted, this sinister goal is not logically possible. The primary impediment, of course, is the fact that central banks today are not privately owned; but are independently-run branches of their respective federal governments. It's the commercial and investment banks of a nation that are privately owned.

Nor is the BIS privately owned today. Originally, however, the BIS was owned by both central banks *and* private individuals, because the United States, Belgium and France sold some or all of their original central-bank shares to private investors. Moreover, even though BIS shares were once traded on stock markets, these were all later repurchased; such that the BIS is now wholly owned by its central-bank members. Any profits accrued from BIS banking transactions are re-invested into its own international activities.

The BIS, then, is currently owned by 60 central banks from around the world that are answerable to their own national governments.[24] Moreover, except for the Peoples Bank of China, the Hong Kong Monetary Authority, the Saudi Arabian Monetary Agency and the Central Bank of the United Arab Emirates, all the central banks of the BIS are legislatively controlled by democratic governments. Hence, the BIS is obviously not controlled by a secretive and private financial elite. For the BIS to covertly control the entire world economy would therefore require the conspiratorial collusion of 60 governmentally-controlled central banks! Such is highly unlikely to occur.

Moreover, the fact that the world's central banks have their own overarching central bank is not necessarily a nefarious idea. Since today's national economies are so globally intertwined with international monetary institutions already in existence (such as the World Bank and the International Monetary Fund), it makes perfect sense for the world's competing national central banks to meet regularly, and to try and coordinate their efforts in attempting to maintain a stable world economy.

It is certainly true that the BIS enjoys special status in a number of areas. For example, all of the bank's archives, documents and data media are "inviolable at all times and in all places." More specifically, the BIS has the right to communicate in code and to travel with embassy-like bags that cannot be searched (except on evidence of criminality). Also similar to embassies, Swiss authorities cannot enter BIS buildings without the management's permission; and the

Bank's assets are not subject to civil claims under Swiss law, nor can they be unilaterally seized. Moreover, officers and employees do not pay income tax on their salaries; and all bank officials under Swiss law are immune, for life, for all actions committed in the exercise of their banking duties. Lastly, the BIS has its own private police force, its own in-house medical facility, and its own bomb shelter (in case of a terrorist attack or armed assault).

Overly-suspicious critics regard all this special status as evidence that the BIS operates above the law, disregarding the fact that all these extraordinary privileges were granted by the intergovernmental agreement of the founding countries, by the 1936 Brussels Protocol with the contracting states, and by the 1987 Headquarters Agreement with the Swiss government. In other words, the BIS operates *within* the context of international and Swiss law, not *above* it.

Also in connection with the BIS, many of these same critics regard anonymity and confidentiality as clear indications of sinister secrecy. While the BIS for many years maintained a low public profile (it originally operated out of an inconspicuous, abandoned hotel in Basel), since 1977 its location and presence have become much more publically visible being headquartered in an eye-catching, eighteen-story circular skyscraper—sarcastically referred to as the "Tower of Basel."

The fact that BIS meetings and conferences are confidential and not open to the public should come as no surprise, given the sensitive nature of monetary policy decisions that crucially affect millions of lives. Democratic governments place their trust and confidence in the autonomous decisions of their central banks. If that trust is ever lost, then there are often several oversight protections to correct it.

In spite of all the alarmism generated by conspiracy theorists, in the case of the BIS, the organization is hardly as secretive as critics like to allege. The BIS has a detailed and informative website that includes annual reports and policy papers that are all downloadable. The Bank's archives and documents are also openly available to outside researchers.

Nevertheless, since there are sinister financial globalists active in the world today (such as George Soros) who conspire to influence international agencies in order to promote their own undemocratic personal agendas, it's always a wise preventative to have independent "watchdog" groups and individuals carefully monitoring the activities of powerful financial organizations such as the Bank for International Settlements.

3.7.8 Goldman Sachs and its Transnational Tentacles of Financial Greed

Unlike central banks, investment banks and commercial banks are not federally established to promote the common good or the public interest; but rather the exclusive self-interest of employees and investors to make money. For many, the investment bank[25] that best exemplifies a "pathological pursuit of profit" is the notorious Goldman Sachs (GS). As memorably described by Matt Taibbi in a 2009 *Rolling Stone* article entitled "The Great American Bubble Machine":

> The first thing you need to know about Goldman Sachs is that it's everywhere. The world's most powerful investment bank is a great vampire squid wrapped around the face of humanity, relentlessly jamming its blood funnel into anything that smells like money.

Originally founded in New York in 1869 by German immigrant Marcus Goldman (1821–1904)—who later partnered in 1882 with his son-in-law Samuel Sachs (1851–1935)—Goldman Sachs is certainly a shrewd and canny survivor despite a constant litany of scandalous behaviour throughout its history. The key to GS's survival—especially in today's global economy—is its ubiquity: Goldman Sachs employees and loyal alumni are everywhere placed in positions of financial power and influence around the world. The unwritten maxim of success for GS is the opposite of the old Rothschild formula—instead of "Control a nation's money supply, and you'll control the nation's government"; it's "Influentially place enough GS loyalists in positions of power, and you'll continue to survive and make enormous profits."

This profiteering survival strategy was glaringly evident during the 2007–2008 international banking crisis. Goldman Sachs was a devious instigator of this worldwide financial meltdown by knowingly dumping bundles of bad mortgage loans (euphemistically called "mortgage-backed securities (MBS)" onto the global market. Knowing these to be toxic loans, GS duplicitously insured itself against their failure with AIG (American International Group), the world's largest insurance company at that time. Moreover, to deceptively market these poisonous MBSs, Standard & Poor's and Moody's—the US's largest credit rating agencies—colludingly gave them AAA ratings.

During the period of the subprime mortgage crisis, three Goldman Sachs alumni were in key positions of financial power and influence in the United States. Hank Paulson, who was the US Treasury Secretary at that time, was previously a partner, chairman and chief executive officer of Goldman Sachs. Neel Kashkari, who was the interim Assistant Secretary of the Treasury for Financial Stability that oversaw TARP (the Troubled Asset Relief Program), had previously worked under Paulson at Goldman Sachs as well. Stephen Friedman, who chaired the New York Federal Reserve Board at that time, was previously a partner, co-chief operating officer and chairman of Goldman Sachs.

When Goldman Sachs went belly-up during the financial meltdown, it didn't crash and burn like Bear Stearns, Lehman Brothers or Merrill Lynch. Instead, GS cunningly morphed itself from being a longtime "investment bank" into suddenly becoming a "bank holding company." By doing so, GS opportunely qualified to receive $10 billion in bailout money from the U.S. Treasury through TARP. Moreover, when insurance giant AIG undeservingly procured government bailout money totaling $182 billion, $13 billion was immediately transferred to Goldman Sachs for the insurance that it had previously taken out against mortgage loan failure. As a result, GS's own subprime losses amounted to a paltry $1.5 billion. Once the $10 billion TARP bailout was paid back with generous interest, Goldman Sachs walked away from their orchestrated subprime loan debacle with a tidy profit—enough to pay its employees more than $20 billion in year-end bonuses in 2009.

Even from a cursory examination of Goldman Sachs' profiteering survival during the 2007–2008 financial crisis, one can clearly discern the invisible hand of ex-GS loyalists moving in high places. Moreover, as a transnational investment bank, Goldman Sachs continues to extend its pernicious money-sucking reach across the globe. The following are some GS alumni who currently (2018) occupy key positions of financial influence in various parts of the world.

Mario Draghi, the current president of the European Central Bank (and previous governor of the Bank of Italy), previously worked for Goldman Sachs International as vice-chairman and managing director. Petros Christodoulou, the Deputy Chief Executive Officer of the National Bank of Greece, previously worked for Goldman Sachs in London and Canada. Mark Carney, the governor of the Bank of England (and former governor of the Bank of Canada), worked at GS for 13 years. Michael Cohrs and Ben

Broadbent, who are also on the Bank of England's board of directors, are both GS veterans. Malcolm Turnbull, the prime minister of Australia, was a former partner of Goldman Sachs. Romano Prodi, who was twice prime minister of Italy, briefly worked as a consultant for Goldman Sachs. Prodi's Treasury undersecretary of the Ministry of Economy and Finance in 2006 was Massimo Tononi, a five-year veteran of Goldman Sachs. Olusegun Olutoyin Aganga, who previously served as Nigeria's minister of finance and then more recently as the minister of industry, trade and investment, was once the managing director of Goldman Sachs International's hedge funds division in London.

Perhaps not surprisingly as well, even the administration of new US President Donald Trump has included a couple of highly-placed GS alumni. The current US Treasury Secretary, Steve Mnuchin, worked at Goldman Sachs for 17 years, eventually becoming chief information officer. Gary Cohn, the director of the National Economic Council (NEC) from January 2017 to April 2018, was previously the president and chief operating officer of Goldman Sachs.

Even though Goldman Sachs has often been chided as "The Bank that Rules the World," their stated core mission is obviously not world rulership; but rather, global profit-making. As a banking behemoth, it doesn't appear to be engaged or interested in government overthrow or usurpation (like George Soros); but seems to be quite content to "help local, state and national governments finance their operations" as a way of making huge piles of money for their employees, clients and investors.

The fact that Goldman Sachs barely survived the 2007-2008 financial meltdown by the skin of its corporate teeth is a good indicator that not even it is "too big to fail," or is totally immune to the powerful economic forces that are globally active today.

3.8 Francis I: A Jesuit Pope with an International Leftist Agenda

As the spiritual leader of 1.2 billion Catholics around the world, Pope Francis I has considerable international influence. However, unlike his two predecessors St. John Paul II and Benedict XVI, Pope Francis is not a "traditional, conservative" Catholic; but rather a "liberal, left-leaning" Catholic. In fact, Pope Francis is better characterized as a "closet socialist" and "communist sympathizer."

While the Pope's constant emphasis on the "plight of the poor" has endeared him to many religious believers as clear evidence of his Christian social charity, the atheistic-left has also surprisingly taken to Francis as a fellow social-justice warrior. What many don't realize is that Pope Francis' preoccupation with the issue of social poverty stems from his admitted admiration of "liberation theology."

This isn't necessarily surprising considering that before he became Pope Francis, Jorge Bergoglio was born and raised in Buenos Aires, Argentina. After becoming a Jesuit in 1960, Bergoglio later became Archbishop of Buenos Aires in 1998, and then cardinal in 2001. Throughout the 1950s and 1960s, many prominent clergy throughout Latin America —particularly Jesuits—formulated, actuated and promulgated a heterodox adulteration of Catholic theology and Marxist ideology known as the "theology of liberation."

Briefly described, liberation theology accepts the faulty materialistic notion of fundamental Marxism that human social history is nothing more than ongoing class warfare; that is, a continual struggle between the oppressive, ruling-class, wealthy "bourgeoisie" and the oppressed, working-class, poor "proletariat." Accordingly, true happiness on earth can only be achieved by the "liberation" of the oppressed poor, through the revolutionary overthrow of the wealthy ruling-class.

Catholic theology regarding God, Jesus Christ, salvation, heaven, hell, good, evil and the mission of the Church is then parachuted into the context of Marxist class conflict; and presto—out pops liberation theology. Not surprisingly in this communist context, Christ-Jesus is not celebrated as the God-anointed Messiah of spiritual salvation; but rather as a social-justice revolutionary of economic liberation.

The term "liberation theology" was originally coined by Gustavo Gutiérrez, a Peruvian Dominican priest who wrote one of the movement's most influential books, *A Theology of Liberation* (1971). While Gutiérrez himself wasn't personally censored by the Church (though he was instructed by the Vatican to revise some of his more objectionable ideas), liberation theology was strongly and publically condemned by both St. John Paul II and Benedict XVI.

Prior to becoming Pope Benedict, Cardinal Joseph Ratzinger as the head of the Congregation for the Doctrine of the Faith (CDF), unequivocally stated that: "An analysis of the phenomenon of liberation theology reveals that it constitutes a fundamental threat to the faith of the Church." The preponderant elements of Marxist ideology that suffuse liberation theology were especially castigated and condemned.

From the very beginnings of Marxist ideology, the Catholic Church has vehemently opposed both communism and its transitional stage, socialism. Pius IX in 1849, only one year after *The Communist Manifesto* was published by Marx and Engels, described communism and socialism in his encyclical *Nostis et Nobiscum* as "perverted theories" and "pernicious fictions." Leo XIII, soon after in *Quod Apostolici Muneris* (1878), defined communism as "the fatal plague which insinuates itself into the very marrow of human society only to bring about its ruin."

Later in 1931, Pius XI in *Quadragesimo Anno* forcefully stated: "Religious socialism, Christian socialism, are contradictory terms; no one can be at the same time a good

Catholic and a true socialist." He was even fiercer in *Divini Redemptoris* (1937), declaring that communism was a "truly diabolical" instrument of "the sons of darkness."

Then shockingly, after more than a century and a half of unvarnished, unambiguous Church opposition to communism, along comes Pope Francis who in a 2016 interview with Italian journalist Eugenio Scalfari responded to the question:

> So you yearn for a society where equality dominates. This, as you know, is the programme of Marxist-socialism and then of communism. Are you therefore thinking of a Marxist type of society?

—with the astonishing answer:

> It has been said many times and my response has always been that, if anything, *it is the communists who think like Christians* [emphasis added]. Christ spoke of a society where the poor, the weak and the marginalized have the right to decide. Not demagogues, not Barabbas, but the people, the poor, whether they have faith in a transcendent God or not. It is they who must help to achieve equality and freedom.

Without a doubt, then, from the statement quoted above and from the fact that Francis has knowingly repeated it several times, the present Pope is an admitted "communist sympathizer." Moreover, even prior to becoming Pope, Francis was erroneously equating the Gospels and the Church Fathers with communism, as evident from the following 2010 quotation:

> The option for the poor comes from the first centuries of Christianity. It's the Gospel itself. If you were to read one of the sermons of the first fathers of the Church, from the second or third centuries, about how you should treat the poor, you'd say it was Maoist or Trotskyist.[26] The

Church has always had the honor of this preferential
option for the poor ...

Not only is the preceding quotation a further indication of
Francis' pro-communist sympathy; but also his intellectual
embrace of liberation theology. His laudatory use of the
phrase, "preferential treatment of the poor" does not come
from the Bible or from Patristic writings;[27] but rather, from
liberation theology. While helping the poor is certainly a part
of Christian social charity, it is hardly "the Gospel itself" as
Francis declares. The Church has always taught that the
central message of the Gospels is the spiritual salvation of
sinful humanity through the life, death and resurrection of
Jesus Christ; not the economic liberation of the poor through
the revolutionary overthrow of the ruling-class.

Moreover, concerning Francis' feigned, lukewarm
opposition to liberation theology when he was Archbishop of
Buenos Aires, it's clear that what Francis was rightly opposed
to in Latin America was the violent, military application of
liberation theology—*not* the communist ideology that
underpinned liberation theology—especially its Marxist
emphasis on liberating the poor and oppressed. One cannot
praise liberation theology for its preferential concern for the
poor, and then claim to reject its Marxist elements—as Francis
has done.[28] Without the Marxist notion of a historical class
struggle, there *is* *no* emphasis on liberating the poor in
liberation theology.

Once it is clearly understood that Pope Francis is an
admitted communist sympathizer and a vocal proponent of
liberation theology, then much of his puzzling (to Catholic
traditionalists) socialist-style behaviour and pronouncements
makes perfectly-logical sense. This explains why Francis
smilingly accepted a blasphemous wooden sculpture of Christ
crucified on a hammer and sickle from Bolivian socialist
president, Evo Morales in 2015. This disturbing "symbol of
liberation theology" had been created by radical, Spanish-

born Bolivian Jesuit, Luis Espinal (1932–1980).

Francis' intellectual espousal of liberation theology also explains why he invited Gustavo Gutiérrez, the Dominican "father of liberation theology," to the Vatican only six months after he became pope. It also explains why Francis lifted a 29-year Vatican suspension on Miguel D'Escoto Brockman (1933–2017), a Maryknoll priest who collaborated as foreign minister for 11 years with the brutally-repressive Sandinista communist government in Nicaragua.[29]

Francis' socialist ideology also explains his expletive diatribes of "savage capitalism" and the free-market economy. In one instance, he colourfully described the "unfettered pursuit of money" as the "the dung of the devil." In another instance, Francis described "the world market" (that is, capitalism) as "an idolatrous economy" that "runs counter to the plan of Jesus." In a 2015 speech in Bolivia, Francis further stated:

> Once capital becomes an idol and guides people's decisions, once greed for money presides over the entire socioeconomic system, it ruins society, it condemns and enslaves men and women, it destroys human fraternity, it sets people against one another and, as we clearly see, it even puts at risk our common home.

As all-to-evident in the 2007–2008 financial meltdown, the corruption and manipulation of free-market capitalism unquestionably causes unjust and widespread harm to the innocent lives of many. But when capitalism has historically operated fairly and equitably, it has positively raised the living conditions of countless individuals in poverty. When Francis decries the negative excesses and injustices of capitalism without acknowledging the positive benefits of lawful and legitimate capitalism, he condemns the entire financial system in true Marxist fashion.

In only five years into his papacy, countlessly-more

examples of Francis' words and behaviour could be listed here as evidence of his socialist worldview. But such is unnecessary from the definitive examples already presented. So what does a socialist pope mean for the Catholic Church and for the world?

Unfortunately for Catholicism, a socialist pope means an imposed socialist agenda on the universal Church. While numerous liberal, left-wing members within the Church endorse and support such a socialist agenda;[30] far-greater traditional, conservative members will strongly reject and resist any socialist subversion.[31] The result could very well be a serious split or "schism" within the Church. In fact, in a 2016 *Der Spiegel* article by Walter Mayr, Pope Francis is purported to have acknowledged this possible division:

> In a very small circle, Pope Francis is said to have self-critically further explained himself as follows: "It is not to be excluded that I will enter history as the one who split the Catholic Church."

Additionally divisive for the Catholic Church, as more and more ecclesiastical members—laity, priests, monastics, bishops and cardinals—strongly contend with Pius XI that "Religious socialism, Christian socialism, are contradictory terms; no one can be at the same time a good Catholic and a true socialist"; then more and more members will dismiss, disregard and disobey Francis as a "non-Catholic pope," or a "false pope," or an "anti-pope."[32]

As to Francis' socialist agenda for the Catholic Church, judging by his leftist rhetoric, he intends to use his autocratic power as supreme pontiff to transform the hierarchical Church into "the People's Church." According to liberation theology, the hierarchical Church is a part of the oppressive ruling-class, and must therefore be overthrown through revolutionary means. If Francis had full sway (which thankfully he hasn't), "Christ's Church for All his People" would become "the People's Church for All the Religions." Where international political socialists strive for a one-world government and military; and international financial socialists strive for a one-world currency and central bank; international religious socialists strive for a one-world religion—and for Francis, that universal religion would be an impoverished Catholic Church[33] that was denominationally all-inclusive—embracing all faiths such as Islam, Judaism, Protestantism, Hinduism, Orthodox and Buddhism.

Aside from Francis' own distorted dream of creating a universal socialist Church,[34] not surprisingly, he has captured the attention of other left-wing globalists[35]—particularly the infamous multi-billionaire, George Soros. Even though he's an atheist, Soros is more than willing to infiltrate and use the worldwide outreach and influence of the Catholic Church to deviously further his own globalist agenda to establish a one-world socialist state.

On a national level, in an effort to radically sway Catholic social policy in America and to influence undecided Catholic voters to support left-wing politicians, Soros covertly funds a number of bogus, pseudo-Catholic groups such as Catholics in Alliance for the Common Good, Catholics United, and Catholics for Choice. Contrary to Catholic doctrine and canon law, these fraudulent organizations actively or surreptitiously work to promote abortion as an acceptable moral choice in society.

On an international level, Soros has planted a number of leftist operatives in the United Nations and in the Vatican. Moreover, as a socialist ideologue himself, Pope Francis has opened wide the Vatican research doors to exclusively-leftist advice on environmentalism, climate change, immigration and economics. One such Soros operative is economist, Jeffrey Sachs, the current special advisor to the UN secretary general on "Millennium Development Goals" (which have been praised by Pope Francis).[36] While at the Vatican, Sachs and other Soros minions produced a radical climate change manifesto entitled "Climate Change and our Common Home," which served as the blueprint for Francis' socialist-style encyclical on the environment, *Laudato Si* (2015).

Another long-time Soros collaborator and consultant is former chief economist of the World Bank, Joseph Stiglitz. Stiglitz co-founded and currently heads the Soros-funded think-tank, Initiative for Policy Dialogue, which promotes "a new international currency" and a global taxation system. Stiglitz is also a member of the Pontifical Academy of Social Sciences, where he helped write the "Climate Change" eco-manifesto with Jeffrey Sachs and others. Not surprisingly, he is also a member of the Socialist International.

Stiglitz has had his socialist fingers in United Nations activities as well. In 2009, then President of the UN General Assembly, Miguel D'Escoto Brockmann—the Catholic priest who was long-suspended for being a Nicaraguan minister in the communist Sandinista government—appointed Stiglitz as the chairman of the UN Commission on Reforms of the International Monetary and Financial System, where he commissioned *The Stiglitz Report.*

While more Soros operatives in the Vatican could be identified, just Sachs and Stiglitz alone sufficiently indicate the extent of Soros' influence on the current, Catholic social policy of Pope Francis. No doubt Soros and his fellow one-world globalists smugly celebrate the acquisition of a socialist pope to bolster their insidious agenda with moral and religious backing. As succinctly stated by international child-protection advocate Elizabeth Yore in a 2016 article entitled "The Pope's Boss":

> George Soros could not have imagined a more perfect partner on the world stage, one he has been searching for his entire career: a major religious leader pontificating as the moral authority for the environmental, borderless countries, mass migration, and pro-Islamic movements.

Unfortunately for Soros, as a non-Catholic he is obviously unaware that Catholics are not obliged to accept Francis' letters, exhortations, encyclicals, homilies or off-hand remarks. As more and more traditional Catholics become aware of Francis' socialist agenda for the Church and for the world, they will simply reject his heterodox ramblings and the globalist infiltrations of the Soros operatives in the Vatican.

3.9 A Rational Analysis of the New World Order (NWO) and One-World Government

3.9.1 Background Introduction to New World Order

Unfortunately today, the mere mention of the "New World Order" conjures up a bizarre and outlandish variety of conspiracy theories; some involving extraterrestrials (the "Reptilians," the "Greys"), or Freemasons, or Jewish financiers (the Rothschilds, the Goldmans, the Warburgs, the Lazards, the Lehmans, etc.), or occult societies (the Illuminati, the Great White Brotherhood), or Nazis (the "Fourth Reich"), or globalist think-tanks (the Council on Foreign Relations, the Trilateral Commission), or the "Red Menace" (international communism), or the end-time Antichrist (Satan).

The problem with all these irrational theories is that they tend to obfuscate, conceal and distort any reasonable understanding and assessment of the present-day meaning of the New World Order. Fact is, the idea of a "new world order" has changed over the centuries, and has meant different things to different people.

Obviously such a notion as a "world order," that is: a system, society, government, organization or arrangement—involving the entire world—is a modern concept. In ancient times, so-called "world empires," no matter how extensive, only involved localized areas of the earth—not the entire planet (see sub-chapter 3.1). A concept such as a world order was not feasible until worldwide travel and communication was established during the Age of Exploration (which began in the fifteenth century and which culminated in the eighteenth century).

3.9.2 Early-American Freemasonry and the New World Order

The concept and the phrase, "New World Order," actually originated in the 1700s with American Freemasonry. Amazingly, few people today realize the deeply-profound influence that Freemasonry has had in historically shaping the American Republic from the very beginning until today. Many prominent and influential statesmen and leaders of the early Republic were Freemasons: George Washington, Benjamin Franklin, Steve Austin, Davy Crockett, Jim Bowie, John Hancock, Patrick Henry, Sam Houston and Paul Revere.

Many of the iconic buildings, statues, monuments, landmarks and symbols that have helped define the United States of America are connected with Freemasonry as well. One such famous example is the Statue of Liberty in New York Harbour. In 1884, "Lady Liberty" was presented as a gift to the Freemasons of America from the Grand Orient Freemasons of France. Moreover, the statue was designed by French Freemason, Frédéric Bartholdi (1834–1904); and built by fellow French Freemason, Gustave Eiffel (1832–1923).[37]

One of the world's best-known architectural structures, the U.S. Capitol Building in Washington, D.C., is steeped in Masonic history as well. The laying of the cornerstone for the original building in 1793 was a full Masonic ceremony conducted by US President and Freemason, George Washington, under the auspices of the Grand Lodge of

Maryland. Furthermore, the building was designed and built by a succession of architects who were almost all Freemasons.

Although the Capital Building was originally designed by non-Mason William Thornton (1759–1828), the work was completed by Freemason Benjamin Latrobe (1764–1820), who also redesigned it after the War of 1812. The north and south wings of the building and the great central dome were later added by Freemason Thomas Ustick Walter (1804–1887).

Another equally-iconic American building is, of course, the official residence and workplace of US presidents—the White House in Washington, D.C. This world-famous structure was designed and built by Freemason James Hoban (1762?–1831). Hoban supervised the construction and laid the cornerstone of the first White House in 1792. After the fiery destruction of the original building during the War of 1812, he also designed much of the present-day building.

Masonic inspiration also explains the enigmatic presence of an enormous, Egyptian-style obelisk on the National Mall in Washington, D.C., known as the Washington Monument. Masonic art, architecture, symbolism and ritual have historically been heavily influenced by ancient Egyptian civilization and culture—well-attested to by the magnificent, sphinx-guarded House of the Temple in Washington, D.C.—the headquarters of the Scottish Rite of Freemasonry, Southern Jurisdiction.

Not surprisingly, then, the original design for the Washington Monument was done by Freemason Robert Mills (1781–1855). Moreover, on July 4, 1848, the cornerstone of the Monument was symbolically (not physically) laid with elaborate Masonic ceremonies.

Another world-famous, but highly-unusual American iconic monument is the Mt. Rushmore National Memorial situated in the Black Hills of South Dakota. It has the largest figures of any statue in the world; and was designed and executed by Freemason Gutzon Borglum (1871–1941). The massive sculpture depicts the 60-foot heads of four U.S. presidents: George Washington (1732–1799), Thomas Jefferson (1743–1826), Theodore Roosevelt (1858–1919), and Abraham Lincoln (1809–1865).

Interestingly as well, both presidents Washington and Roosevelt are officially-acknowledged Freemasons. Lincoln, on the other hand, had applied for Masonic membership in Tyrian Lodge, Springfield, Ill.; but withdrew the application shortly after his presidential nomination in 1860, so as not to be accused of "vote-getting." And although Jefferson is not undisputedly regarded as a Freemason, he was known to have attended Masonic meetings, marched in a Masonic procession, participated in a Masonic cornerstone ceremony, had a Masonic lodge chartered in his name before he died, and had Masonic funeral rites and processions performed for him.[38] So, applying the "duck test" of abductive reasoning: "If it walks like a duck, quacks like a duck ..."

It seems rather amazing, then, that given Freemasonry's enormous political influence and highly-visible achievements throughout American society that one of its greatest symbols is everywhere present, nowhere noticed and hardly anywhere understood. That profound symbol is the unfinished pyramid capped with the radiant, all-seeing eye of God.

This arcane, mystic symbol of Freemasonry forms the reverse of the Great Seal of the United States, and is also found on the back of the American one-dollar bill (please refer to the back cover of this book). Many historians (including Masonic ones) reject that this is a Masonic symbol, based mainly on the fact that all of the recognized designers of the Great Seal were non-Masons (except for Benjamin Franklin, who directed the first design committee in 1776).

Unfortunately, this erroneous conclusion fails to acknowledge that the professional designers of the Great Seal could very well have been artistically inspired by anonymous, influential Masons. Logically considered, why else would an uncapped, Egyptian-style pyramid that closely resembles the Great Pyramid of Giza[39] appear in an important early-American design if it didn't come from the Egyptian symbolism prominently found in American Freemasonry? This same reasoning convincingly explains why there is a gigantic, Egyptian-style obelisk in Washington, D.C. as well.

Similar faulty reasoning has been used to dismiss the eye of God (above the uncapped pyramid) as another, well-recognized Masonic symbol. While Masons readily admit that the all-seeing eye of God (which they also term the "eye of providence") is a familiar Masonic symbol today, some argue that it wasn't a Masonic symbol in 1782 when the Great Seal design was completed. Because of this, they argue, the reverse of the Great Seal cannot possibly be a Masonic design.

The problem with this argument is—it isn't factually correct. The Director of Communications and Development of The George Washington Masonic National Memorial Association, Shawn E. Eyer, has provided the following ample evidence that the all-seeing eye was associated with Freemasonry well before 1782:

> [I]t is easy to see that the All-Seeing Eye would have been a familiar symbol to the early Freemasons.
>
> The earliest example of such a symbol just might be on a personal seal of Bro. Robert Moray (1609–1673) ... A partial wax impression of one of his seals is in the shape of a circle, with an eye at the center, radiating in every direction to the circumference.
>
> The symbol appears in an unmistakable way in the engraved frontispieces of two books of Bro. Fifield D'Assingy (1707–1744) ... Each depicts the All-Seeing Eye with rays descending ...
>
> [I]n the 1770s, during the ascendancy of the great Masonic lecturer, Bro. William Preston (1742–1818). The

symbol appears in numerous places and forms in Preston's degree lectures ...

In 1766, Bro. Isaac Head gave a Charge in the Scilly Isles of England, in which he asked that the brethren remain "ever mindful that the Eye which pervades the immeasurable Regions of Space, and sees through the thickest Darkness, is ever present with us."

It should be noted here as well that the all-seeing eye is not exclusively a Masonic symbol; but was in fact appropriated from the Catholic Church. One of the earliest Church depictions of the all-seeing eye within a triangle is in the Palatine Chapel in Aachen, which was built in 786 by Charlemagne. As understood by the early Church, the eye in the triangle symbolized "one God in three divine persons (the Trinity)."

Throughout history, the brotherhood of stonemasons regarded their gifted profession as involving more than just building monumental stone structures; such as the Egyptian pyramids, Solomon's Temple, medieval castles or Renaissance cathedrals. As spectacular as these constructions were, they were regarded as the "lesser work." The "great work" was seen as positively contributing to human progress and civilization through their worldly endeavors and obedience to God. During the more philosophically-inclined Age of Enlightenment, these fraternal beliefs took on a more artistic, symbolic form as the uncapped pyramid with the all-seeing eye above

As understood and applied by the Freemasonic Founding Fathers and their revolutionary brethren, then, the uncapped pyramid symbolized their "great work" of building a more perfect society under God in the New World; that is, of breaking away from the British monarchy of the Old World and establishing a democratic republic, "with a firm reliance on the protection of Divine Providence."[40]

The American Freemasonic ideal "to form a more perfect

Union"[41] (or social order) under God—that is symbolized on the reverse of the Great Seal—is also conveyed in the Latin mottos above and below the unfinished pyramid and all-seeing eye. The Latin words "Annuit Coeptis" in the sky above the pyramid translates as "He [God] favors our undertakings." The words "Novus Ordo Seclorum" in a scroll below the pyramid correctly translates as "New World Order."[42] Together, the Latin words convey: "God blesses the establishing of our social Order in the New World." The two Latin phrases, then, mirror and reinforce the symbolic meaning of the unfinished pyramid and all-seeing eye of the Great Seal.

It's obvious, then, (except to some hardened conspiracy theorists) that the early-American Masonic use of the motto, "New World Order," in no way indicates a nefarious Masonic scheme for world domination. Quite the opposite, in fact; as originally understood it celebrated the birth of a new, sovereign, democratic nation that was fervently opposed to governmental tyranny, despotism and authoritarianism.

3.9.3   Woodrow Wilson and his Visionary New World Order following World War I

Once the early-American motto, "New World Order," became more widely known within Masonic circles, it also became more familiar to non-Masons who would unfortunately use the phrase to mean entirely different things. Such was the case with US President Woodrow Wilson (1856–1924). In a joint session of Congress in 1918, Wilson referred to a "new international order" and a "new order [for] the world," as in the following:

> We believe that our own desire for a new international order under which reason and justice and the common interests of mankind shall prevail is the desire of enlightened men everywhere. Without that new order the

world will be without peace and human life will lack tolerable conditions of existence and development. Having set our hand to the task of achieving it, we shall not turn back.

For Wilson, the "new world order" was an idealist vision to establish improved international relations in order to end World War I, and to prevent another devastating worldwide conflict from recurring in the future. To achieve this goal, Wilson formulated a 14-point program for world peace, which included a proposal to establish "a general association of nations"—an international "League of Nations."

Without strong governmental support from America's three major European allies in World War I—Britain, France and Italy—and without the support of the US Senate, Wilson's Fourteen Points were doomed to failure. Moreover, the peace Treaty of Versailles that ended the Great War in 1919 bore little resemblance to the Fourteen Points. This fact, and the impossible reparations payments imposed on Germany, would later contribute to the rise of Nazism, and the eventuality of a second world war.

As for Wilson's League of Nations, although it was actually established by the Paris Peace Conference in 1920, it only lasted until 1946. Ironically, since the real purpose of the League of Nations was to dilute national sovereignty and to replace it with a global government, the United States never joined. Moreover, the Soviet Union only briefly joined; and later, Germany, Japan, Italy, Spain and others withdrew from the League. Obviously, since the League of Nations was established to prevent future international conflict, the outbreak of World War II proved Wilson's League of Nations to be an international failure as well.

Even though Wilson's visionary "new world order" was never fully realized, the historical fact is that by the end of the First World War the Old World political order had actually been radically alterred.[43] The Austro-Hungarian, Russian and

German Empires were gone. Most of the European monarchies had been swept away. Though the colonial British Empire was still geographically extensive, in the immediate aftermath of World War I, Britain was no longer the world's pre-eminent military or industrial power; the United States and Germany had begun to seriously challenge Britain's economic superiority.

3.9.4 Roosevelt and Churchill: A Different New World Order following World War II

With the failure of Wilson's visionary conception of a new world order after the First World War, the phrase was little used until the aftermath of World War II. Once again during the post-war years there was talk of a new world order; but one that was noticeably different than Wilson's vision. In both cases, however, the driving motivation was to somehow improve international relations to prevent another world war from occurring.

Once again, the main proponent of a new world order was an American president; in this instance, Franklin D. Roosevelt (1882–1945). As a Freemason himself, Roosevelt was quite familiar with the Masonic motto, "Novus Ordo Seclorum"; that is, "New World Order." In fact, it was President Roosevelt who decided in 1935 to put both sides of the Great Seal on the reverse of the American one-dollar bill. As described by Secretary of Agriculture Henry A. Wallace in letters written in 1951 and in 1955:

> Turning to page 53 [in a State Department publication entitled, *The History of the Seal of the United States*] I noted the colored reproduction of the reverse side of the Seal. The Latin phrase "Novus Ordo Seclorum" impressed me as meaning the "New Deal of the Ages."
>
> I was struck by the fact that the reverse side of the Seal had never been used. Therefore I took the publication to

President Roosevelt and suggested a coin be put out with the obverse and reverse sides of the Seal.

Roosevelt, as he looked at the colored reproduction of the Seal, was first struck with the representation of the "All Seeing Eye," a Masonic representation of The Great Architect of the Universe [God]. Next he was impressed with the idea that the foundation for the new order of the ages had been laid in 1776, but that it would be completed only under the eye of the Great Architect. Roosevelt like myself was a 32nd degree Mason.

He suggested that the Seal be put on the dollar bill rather than a coin and took the matter up with the Secretary of the Treasury. He brought it up in a Cabinet meeting and asked James Farley [Postmaster General and a Roman Catholic] if he thought the Catholics would have any objection to the "All Seeing Eye" which he as a Mason looked on as a Masonic symbol of Deity. Farley said "no, there would be no objection."

In other words, as Roosevelt saw it, the new world order—the US Republican Order of the New World—that began in 1776, was the outcome of the American War of Independence. Since then, the ideal of a democratically-free, sovereign nation under God had spread to other parts of the world. The new social order that began in America was becoming increasingly worldwide, increasingly international.

Just as the aftermath of the First World War had provided President Wilson with an auspicious environment to try and improve international relations, Roosevelt saw a similar political opportunity to establish a superior international order that would prevent future world wars. As a Freemason, Roosevelt saw the politically-altered, post-war conditions of World War II as a opportune moment in history to continue the "great work" of building a more perfect social order—worldwide.

In a 1940 Armistice Day address before the Tomb of the

Unknown Soldier, Roosevelt detailed some of his own NWO vision:

> We, alive today—not in the existent democracies alone, but also among the populations of the smaller nations already overrun—are thinking in the larger terms of the maintenance of the "New Order" to which we have been accustomed, and in which we intend to continue.
>
> We recognize certain facts of 1940 which did not exist in 1918—a need for the elimination of aggressive armaments—a need for the breaking down of barriers in a more closely knitted world—a need for restoring honor in the written and spoken word.
>
> We recognize that the processes of democracy must be greatly improved, in order that we may attain those purposes.

Likewise, in a speech given in 1941 to a Joint Session of Congress, Roosevelt stated: "The 'World Order' which we seek is the co-operation of free countries, working together in a friendly, civilized society."

As had occurred with World War I, by the end of the Second World War the political landscape of the world had once more been dramatically altered. The United States was now the first nuclear nation and an undisputed superpower among nations. Despite the horrendous loss of life (26.6 million), Russia emerged from the war with a far-increased military capability and increased European territory (the Eastern Bloc states). It would soon emerge as a rival superpower to the U.S.

With the United States continuing to far surpass Great Britain in military might, industrial technology and economic prowess after each world war, then-British prime minister, Winston Churchill (1874–1965), made every effort to preserve a strong post-war alliance with the American superpower. In a 1946 speech given in Fulton, Missouri, entitled "The Sinews of Peace" Churchill stated:

> The United States stands at this time at the pinnacle of world power. It is a solemn moment for the American Democracy ... Opportunity is here now, clear and shining for both our countries...
>
> Neither the sure prevention of war, nor the continuous rise of world organization will be gained without what I have called the fraternal association of the English-speaking peoples. This means a special relationship between the British Commonwealth and Empire and the United States.

Interestingly, even though Churchill was a Freemason for only a short period of time (1901–1912), some of the language expressed in "The Sinews of Peace" sound somewhat Masonic; such as:

> A [new] world organization has already been erected for the prime purpose of preventing war, UNO [the United Nations Organization], the successor of the League of Nations ... I spoke earlier of the Temple of Peace. Workmen from all countries must build that temple.

3.9.5 The Post-War Growth and Spread of the "Liberal World Order (LWO)"

Because the Second World War, out of military necessity, forced the increased transportation of goods and supplies between North America and Europe, between North America and Asia, and amongst all the warring nations in Europe and Asia, during the relatively-peaceful post-war years this resulted in increased international trade and commerce. Similarly, technological wartime advances in intercontinental communication brought the global community much closer together.

Not surprisingly, then, the post-war years were

characterized by the increased globalization of business, trade, industrial production, banking, political alignments, military cooperation and intercontinental travel. Moreover, the intergovernmental push for improved relations between nations as a means of preventing yet another worldwide conflagration resulted in the formation of a number of international institutions and multilateral agreements: the United Nations (1945), the North Atlantic Treaty Organization or NATO (1949), the International Monetary Fund or IMF (1945), the International Bank for Reconstruction and Development or World Bank (1944), the International Agreement on Tariffs and Trade or GATT (1947), the European Recovery Program or ERP (1948), and the International Court of Justice or World Court (1945–46).

This globalized interconnectedness in the aftermath of World War II, developed into what has become known as the "liberal world order (LWO)." As a post-war system of international relations, the liberal world order was predominantly shaped and defined by the leadership of the United States and its Western allies working through the various international institutions. Besides providing a degree of international economic stability, the liberal world order also promoted open markets and free trade, liberal democracy, and free-market capitalism.

Even though the Soviet Union was a founding member of many post-war international institutions, the rapid rise of communist Russian as a rival nuclear superpower to the West put the former wartime ally at serious odds with the burgeoning liberal world order. By providing a formidable balance of power in favour of the United States and allied Western democracies, the liberal world order helped contain the spread of Russian communism, and the possibility of nuclear war between the two opposing superpowers.

Therefore, while the liberal world order was unable to establish complete world peace, for a time it did reduce open global warfare between East and West to a "Cold War" series of small, regional proxy-hostilities around the world. This limited global conflict also became known as the "Pax Americana."

3.9.6 The End of the Cold War and the New World Order of George H.W. Bush

With the dramatic economic collapse and political dissolution of the Soviet Union in 1991, there remained only one superpower on the world stage, the United States of America. As three US presidents had done previously (Washington, Wilson and Roosevelt), George H.W. Bush saw the end of the Cold War as another opportunity to establish a different kind of new world order. In a 1991 address to Congress entitled "Toward a New World Order"[44] Bush Sr. stated:

Now, we can see a new world coming into view. A world in which there is the very real prospect of a new world order. In the words of Winston Churchill, a "world order" in which "the principles of justice and fair play ... protect the weak against the strong ..." A world where the United Nations, freed from cold war stalemate, is poised to fulfill the historic vision of its founders. A world in which freedom and respect for human rights find a home among all nations.

Bush Sr., then, envisioned a new world order where the United States and Russia would work together through the United Nations to establish and maintain international stability and peace. As described by A.M. Rosenthal in an excerpt from the *New York Times* (January 1991):

But it became clear as time went on that in Mr. Bush's mind the New World Order was founded on a convergence of goals and interests between the U.S. and the Soviet Union, so strong and permanent that they would work as a team through the U.N. Security Council.

Interestingly, the vision of a new world order of cooperation between the US and Russia was also shared by then-Soviet leader, Mikhail Gorbachev, even before the end of the Cold War. In an address to the United Nations in 1988 Gorbachev stated: "Further global progress is now possible only through a quest for universal consensus in the movement towards a new world order."[45]

The first major international crisis after the end of the Cold War was the Gulf War of 1990–91, precipitated by the Iraqi invasion and annexation of Kuwait. This would also prove to be the first significant test of any new world order cooperation between the US and Russia. The US-led military operation assembled an unprecedented international coalition of 35 nations, the largest military alliance since World War II.

Even though the Soviet Union had previous, Cold War military ties to Iraq for two decades—training Iraqi troops, and supplying billions of dollars worth of weapons and equipment—it did not stand in opposition to the Gulf War coalition. While Russia did condemn the Iraqi incursion into Kuwait, it did not commit troops; but instead tried unsuccessfully to avoid military action through diplomatic negotiation.

Although Bush Sr. considered the Gulf War to be a positive test of bilateral cooperation in the post-Cold War era, Russia quickly concluded that continued alliance with the United States essentially meant passively complying with American foreign policy. Needless to say, that was not about to happen. The elation that Bush Sr. conveyed to Congress soon after the Gulf War ended, proved to be very short-lived:

> The gulf war put this new world [order] to its, its first test. And my fellow Americans, we passed that test.
>
> The victory over Iraq was not waged as "a war to end

all wars." Even the new world order cannot guarantee an era of perpetual peace. But enduring peace must be our mission.

Our success in the gulf will shape not only the new world order we seek but our mission here at home.

3.9.7 The Economic Inequality of the Liberal World Order as a Pretense for One-World Government

While the liberal world order that was established after the end of World War II proved to be an era of general economic prosperity and stability, this prosperity was not equally shared around the world. The main beneficiaries of the post-war economic boom were the Western democracies, particularly the United States.

Unfortunately, as time went on it became clear that even in the US it was only a small percentage of financial and corporate elites (such as banks, financiers, company executives and multinational corporations) that accrued the largest percentage of the post-war wealth. Worldwide the unequal distribution of wealth continued to exponentially rise.

By 2018, an Oxfam study reported that 82 percent of the wealth generated in 2017 went to the richest 1 percent of the global population, while the 3.7 billion people who made up the poorest half of the world saw no increase in their wealth. It is also estimated that 8.6 percent of the world's population owns 85 percent of the world's wealth; while 70 percent of the world's population owns only 3 percent of the world's wealth.

Eventually, such a glaringly-unequal distribution of global wealth was bound to cause widespread discouragement, discontentment, disillusionment, resentment and anger from the majority of those who are not financially benefiting from the liberal world order. The "Occupy Wall Street" protest movement in 2011 was a recent expression of this growing public discontent.

The global financial meltdown in 2007–2008 highlighted many of the systemic venalities of the liberal world order that permit and perpetuate wealth disparity. Wealthy individuals and corporations, for example, are free to stash their fortunes in off-shore bank accounts in order to avoid paying their fair share of taxes. Multinational companies are also free to lay off workers and close down factories in one country, in order to take advantage of cheap labour in another country. Secretly-negotiated, multinational free-trade agreements grant corporations the undemocratic power to override government safety and environmental laws; and the power to sue interfering governments for any loss of revenue.

Furthermore, wealthy individuals and corporations can bury their money in tax-free foundations; and then use that money to bankroll beholden politicians, or to covertly fund lobby and activist groups that perpetuate their wealth acquisition. Corrupt banks and investment firms, if they're large enough, are protected from self-induced financial collapse through billion-dollar, government-arranged taxpayer bailouts. Similarly, corporations that are large enough can also qualify for "corporate welfare"; that is, government monetary handouts that are granted when they're in serious financial difficulty.

While many more built-in abuses of the present-day, globalized economic and political system—the liberal world order—could easily be detailed, the point here is that unless the increasingly-unfair and unjust global wealth disparity is checked and remedied, international social upheaval is certain to occur. What is worrisome is the fact that in the past, excessive wealth disparity within individual nations has been the root cause for violent revolution; such as the French Revolution in monarchist France, the Bolshevik Revolution in czarist Russia, and the Chinese Revolution in imperial China. Excessive disparity between rich and poor on a multinational scale, then, may well fuel a global revolution.

What is of particular, present-day concern is that there are numerous individuals and agencies with power and influence that are ready and willing to exploit a worldwide economic crisis as a means to institute a one-world government system. Even back in 1950, James Warburg (1896–1969), the financial advisor to Franklin Roosevelt and a member of the Council on Foreign Relations (CFR) unequivocally stated before the US Senate on Foreign Relations that:

> We shall have world government, whether or not we like it. The question is only whether world government will be achieved by consent or by conquest.

Many others have disturbingly echoed this same sentiment. British polymath, Nobel Laureate and Fabian socialist, Bertrand Russell (1872–1970), wrote in *The Impact of Science on Society* (1952) that:

> [E]ducation for a generation will be able to control its subjects securely without the need of armies or policemen ... Educational propaganda, with government help, could achieve this result in a generation. There are, however, two powerful forces opposed to such a policy: one is religion; the other is nationalism ... A scientific world society cannot be stable unless there is a world government.

Albert Einstein (1879–1955) is also purported to have stated:

> In my opinion the only salvation for civilization and the human race lies in the creation of a world government, with security of nations founded upon law. As long as sovereign states continue to have separate armaments and armament secrets, new world wars will be inevitable. (Quoted by Christopher Hamer in *A Global Parliament—Principles of World Federation*; 1998)

Nobel Prize-winning Dutch economist, Jan Tinbergen (1903–1994) likewise wrote in the 1994 *United Nations Development Report* entitled "Global Governance for the 21st Century":

Mankind's problems can no longer be solved by national governments. What is needed is a World Government. This can best be achieved by strengthening the United Nations system. In some cases, this would mean changing the role of UN agencies from advice-giving to implementation.

Strobe Talbot, President Clinton's Deputy Secretary of State, in a 1992 *Time Magazine* article entitled "America Abroad: The Birth of the Global Nation" similarly stated:

In the next [21st] century, nations as we know it will be obsolete; all states will recognize a single global authority and realize national sovereignty wasn't such a great deal after all.

Well-known author and scientist, Isaac Asimov (1920–1992), has also been quoted as stating:

A world government that can channel human efforts in the direction of the great solutions seems desirable, even essential. Naturally, such a world government should be a federal one, with regional and local autonomy safeguarded and with cultural diversity promoted.

Academy Award-winning British actor and writer, Peter Ustinov (1921–2004), made the following statement as well:

World Government is not only possible, it is inevitable; and when it comes, it will appeal to patriotism in its truest sense, in its only sense, the patriotism of humans who love their national heritages so deeply that they wish to preserve them in safety for the common good.

It's clear from the preceding quotations that there has been a wide and diverse range of support for the idea of a one-world government as a possible remedy to the inequities of the liberal world order. In fact, there exists an international organization originally established in 1937—the World Federalist Movement—that is entirely dedicated to establishing a one-world government.[46]

3.9.8 The Widely-Feared, Socialist-Style, World Government Model

The problem with the broad advocacy of a one-world government, however, is that similar to the diverse promotion of a new world order, not everyone shares the same understanding of what world rulership entails. The one particular model that is most feared, abhorred and rejected by conspiracy theorists, political conservatives and traditional Christians alike is the socialist-style, global-governance model.

Under this possible system of world rulership, individual nations would be required to completely surrender their national sovereignty. There would be no nationally-defended borders, only open borders permitting the unrestricted flow of people, trade goods and services. In time, open borders would dissolve all regional and national distinctions of race, religion and culture. Eventually, there would be no distinct European, Chinese, American, African, Indian, or Asian nations; nor would there be Christian, Moslem, Hindu, Buddhist or Jewish nations. All previously-unique nations would become populated with a similar homogenous mixture of world people.

As well, the socialist world government model would establish a centralized world banking system that would determine global monetary policy and exclusively issue a one-world currency. All nations, then, would be required to surrender their independent monetary policies and their national currencies. The socialist world bank would ensure that there would be no unequally-wealthy or unequally-poor nations; thereby leveling any international wealth disparity. All nations would have an equal allotment of wealth and an equal standard of living determined by the world bank (under the direction of the world government).

Sovereign nations would also be required to surrender their independent military capability, to be replaced by an international military force that would strictly maintain worldwide law and order; and thereby prevent any global conflicts from arising. Individual citizens would also be strictly prohibited from owning or using any firearms or assault weapons.

Under this world socialist government there would be an entirely secular social order with a rigid dividing line between "church and state." Religion, then, would be marginalized and state-controlled, as it is in communist China today. Moreover, in order to prevent possible sectarian conflict, only one world religion would be allowed—a diluted ecumenical amalgam of all previously-independent faiths that all believers could agree with.

While radical-socialists would embrace and advance such a dreadful model of one-world government, history has repeatedly demonstrated that socialist/communist governments are unnatural, unrealistic, unhealthy and unworkable. Moreover, all-powerful state-government control has always and everywhere resulted in the despotic, tyrannical and dictatorial control of a small elite over the broad population of subjugated and oppressed citizens. There is no logical reason to think that a future socialist government at the global scale would be any different than any of the failed attempts of socialism at a national level.

3.9.9 The Socialist New World Order and the One-World Socialist Government are One and the Same

Some naïve theorists mistakenly believe that a one-world socialist government is the positive solution to the future possibility of international warfare; to the current problem of sectarian violence and terrorism; to the current outbreaks of religious conflict; and to the current injustice of unfair wealth disparity that have resulted from the systemic flaws of the liberal world order. What they don't realize is that a socialist world government is the logical extension and culmination of this same liberal world order; it is its crowning, miscreant achievement—the socialist new world order—that is rightfully feared and abhorred by conspiracy theorists, political conservatives and traditional Christians alike.

The radical-socialism that has infected Western democracies is clearly labouring towards a one-world socialist government, a socialist new world order. This explains the open-border policy of the socialist Democratic Party in America, the socialist "Eurocrats" in the European Union, and the socialist billionaires such as George Soros. This also explains the fairly-recent, massive importation of Muslim "refugees" into the unprepared Western democracies.

The socialist policy of "multiculturalism," which is touted as a humanitarian way of promoting cultural diversity, is actually intended to undermine the Western democracies as Christian nations. Despite the fact that 69 percent of the US population is Christian, then-Senator Barak Obama in 2006 proudly proclaimed in typically-socialist fashion that:

> Given the increasing diversity of America's population, the dangers of sectarianism have never been greater. Whatever we once were, we are no longer just a Christian nation; we are also a Jewish nation, a Muslim nation, a Buddhist nation, a Hindu nation, and a nation of nonbelievers.

Moreover, to address the unfair wealth disparity between

nations, the radical-socialists in the West, instead of increasing the wealth of poorer nations, actively work to weaken and siphon off the strong economies of the more prosperous nations. In the United States this has been done by allowing millions of illegal immigrants from Mexico, Central America and South America to flood the US job market with cheap labour. Excessive tax regulations have also devastated US employment by driving job-creating corporations out of the country. As well, unaffordable and profligate welfare programs continue to increase the national debt, and thereby weaken the overall economy. Multinational free-trade deals have often produced huge trade deficits for the United States, which has then resulted in fewer American jobs and decreased production of export goods—thereby additionally weakening the US economy.

At first it may appear somewhat puzzling that globalist billionaires such as George Soros, who have greedily acquired their inordinate riches from free-market capitalism, should extol the state-controlled economy of communist China, and embrace the socialist model for a new world order. It makes perfect sense, however, when it is understood that these globalist billionaires intend to be part of the ruling elite of the one-world government. While they intend to level the wealth disparity between the rich and the poor nations of the world, they hypocritically plan on maintaining and protecting their own vastly unequal riches for themselves and for their future generations. In other words, under the socialist new world order, the 1 percent will perpetually continue to own 80 percent of the world's wealth.

Up until 2016, the world-government socialist forces moving toward the leftist new world order were unabatedly steamrolling ahead throughout the Western democracies. What changed in 2016?—the shattering election of Donald J. Trump as US president.

CHAPTER 4

DONALD J. TRUMP: UNLIKELY "WARRIOR OF GOD"

4.1 Unlikely Warriors of God in Past History

4.1.1 Saul of Tarsus becomes St. Paul the Apostle

TWO-TIME PRESIDENTIAL LOSER, Hillary Clinton, continues to be entirely dumbfounded and unable to comprehend just how and why she lost a foolproof election to real-estate developer and political nobody, Donald J. Trump. In her mind she did everything physically possible to win: spent over a billion dollars on her campaign; had the entire mainstream media biased in her favour; had deep-state intelligence officials spying on Trump; had FBI Director James Comey keep her out of jail; had a phony dossier compiled with salacious Russian-intel that could be used to discredit Trump; and had the televised, candidate-debate questions cheatingly slipped to her in advance.

While Hillary may have done everything "physically" possible, as an atheistic-socialist she will never perceive or comprehend that there were powerful "spiritual" forces actively involved in the world-altering, presidential election of Donald Trump. Unfortunately, other Marxist-socialists like herself do not understand or acknowledge that world history has been purposely shaped by powerful spiritual forces, and not randomly formed by physical, materialistic ones.

From a spiritual perspective, then, it will be noted that at certain crucial points in human history, unlikely individuals suddenly appear on the world stage to effect positive change that is critical to progressive human development. In a very real sense, these unique individuals have been raised up and specially prepared by spiritual forces to assume the mantle of responsibility for specific world change. These individuals can truly be described as "warriors of God."

One such outstanding example of an unlikely warrior of God is Saul of Tarsus (c.4 BC–c.65 AD). Born in Asia Minor (present-day Turkey) and raised as a Jewish Pharisee, Saul was a strict observer and practitioner of Mosaic law; and a believer in life after death and the Hebrew Messiah. Saul also had the advantage of Roman citizenship from his father.

As a young man, Saul moved to Jerusalem where he received a first-class education in the school of Gamaliel, one of the foremost rabbis in history. Consequently, Saul was well versed in Hebrew scripture, Mosaic law and Greek philosophy. He was also fluent in Hebrew, Greek and Latin.

As a zealous, well-educated and dedicated Jewish Pharisee, Saul had originally condemned the early Christians as a dangerous, heretical and blasphemous sect. As Saul understood the Hebrew messiah, he would come as a divinely-appointed human being who would assume the throne of King David, raise a formidable army, defeat the enemies of Israel (including Rome), and establish Israel as the foremost nation on earth.

At first, Saul refused to accept that the true messiah—Christ-Jesus—was both human and divine; that he died a horrible, criminal's death on the cross; and that he later rose from the dead and ascended into heaven. As a result, Saul became a committed and enthusiastic persecutor of Christians in and around Jerusalem; zealously hunting them down, imprisoning and killing them. In fact, the first Christian martyr mentioned in the Bible, St. Stephen (c.5 AD–c.34 AD), who was stoned to death—Saul had "approved of killing."

Given this history, it seems rather preposterous and extremely unlikely that Saul of Tarsus would ever become a devoted Christian apostle; or that he would ever become the foremost Christian theologian who would spread the Gospel of Jesus Christ throughout the Roman Empire. But that is exactly what occurred; by later adopting his Roman name, Saul of Tarsus became St. Paul the Apostle—a very unlikely "warrior of God" indeed.

St. Paul's dramatic role-reversal from "zealous persecutor of Christianity" to "zealous promoter of Christianity" was due to religious "conversion"; a profound spiritual experience that totally transforms an individual, and changes their life completely. In St. Paul's case, his conversion from Jewish Pharisee to Christian apostle was a dramatic superphysical occurrence—the perceptual appearance of Christ-Jesus in his radiant resurrected form.

At the time, Paul was on horseback, travelling to Damascus in order to round up fleeing Christians, and then to bring them back to Jerusalem for imprisonment or execution. The appearance of Christ was so radiantly intense that Paul and his fellow travelers fell off their horses; and in Paul's case, he was blinded for three days afterward. As described in the Book of Acts (26:13–16):

> At midday … I saw on the way a light from heaven, brighter than the sun, shining round me and those who journeyed with me. And when we had all fallen to the ground, I heard a voice saying to me in the Hebrew

language, "Saul, Saul, why do you persecute me? ... And I said, "Who are you, Lord?" And the Lord said, "I am Jesus whom you are persecuting. But rise and stand upon your feet; for I have appeared to you for this purpose, to appoint you to serve and bear witness to the things in which you have seen me and to those in which I will appear to you ..."

Having had his mental eyes opened to the truth, and by turning to God through Christ, Saul sincerely repented for his past grievous sins against Christianity; thereby receiving divine forgiveness and sanctification. By doing so, Saul thereafter truly became a new man—St. Paul the Apostle, a "warrior of God." As Paul himself similarly described in Ephesians (4:22–24):

Put off your old nature which belongs to your former manner of life and is corrupt through deceitful lusts, and be renewed in the spirit of your minds, and put on the new nature, created after the likeness of God in true righteousness and holiness.

The conversional change was so deeply-profound and dramatic with St. Paul that, quite understandably at first, he was not trusted or accepted by the Christian disciples in Damascus. But in a very short time, however, his newly-acquired devotion to Christ-Jesus was so genuinely powerful and convincing that even his fellow Jews began plotting to kill him. Predictably, when Paul returned to Jerusalem three years later he was met with a similarly-suspicious and fearful reception. As described in Acts (9:26–29):

And when he had come to Jerusalem he attempted to join the disciples; and they were all afraid of him, for they did not believe that he was a disciple. But Barnabas took him, and brought him to the apostles, and declared to them how on the road he had seen the Lord, who spoke to him, and how at Damascus he had preached boldly in the name of Jesus. So he went in and out among them at Jerusalem, preaching boldly in the name of the Lord.

Soon after his conversion, Paul travelled at first to Arabia; and in particular to Mount Sinai where it is believed he spent considerable time meditating in the desert. Presumably, this is where he received the deep wisdom of the gospel teachings as a direct revelation from the Risen Christ, and not from any human agency.

From the stand-point of nascent Christianity, it was critical to quickly spread the gospel message far and wide while the first-hand experiences and personal testimonials of Christ's apostles were still fresh and alive. Moreover, it was also vital to quickly establish a strong, foundational Christian theology; that is, a clear intellectual comprehension of the profound life and teachings of the true messiah, Christ-Jesus. At the time, there was no one better suited to assume this essential task than St. Paul. Because of this, we better understand why Christ chose to convert Saul, as stated in Acts (9:15): "[H]e [Saul] is a chosen instrument of mine to carry my name before the Gentiles and kings and the sons of Israel ..."

Since Paul had both Jewish and Roman citizenship, and since he was multilingual in Hebrew, Greek and Latin, he was ideally suited for his missionary calling to spread the Christian gospel throughout the Roman Empire—to become the "Apostle to the Gentiles." And since Paul was well–educated in Hebrew scripture and Greek philosophy, and since he possessed a highly-trained intellectual mind, Paul was also the best qualified among the apostles to formulate a foundational Christian theology.

Without the spiritual world directly intervening in world affairs through the person of the resurrected Christ, and thereby "raising up" St. Paul, nascent Christianity would have had much greater difficulty expanding and surviving. Christianity today has been profoundly shaped by the contribution of St. Paul—an unlikely warrior of God.[47]

4.1.2   Joan of Arc: A Teenage Peasant Girl Leads the French Army and Saves France

Another noteworthy example of the spiritual world directly intervening in world affairs and raising up an unlikely warrior of God is Joan of Arc (c.1412–1431). Without the extraordinary intercession of St. Joan, it is certain that the English monarchy would have captured the French throne and established France as a continental English colony. Naturally, this would have completely altered the entire subsequent history of Europe; and would have subverted the influential role that France would play in future world politics.

Clearly, the spiritual forces that guide world evolution were not about to allow this regressive scenario to happen. In St. Joan's case, the spiritual world directly intervened in the form of supersensible visions and messages that began when she was just 13 years old. St. Joan identified these spiritual personages as St. Michael the archangel, St. Catherine of Alexandria (c.287–c.305) and St. Margaret of Antioch (289–304). They instructed her to drive the English out of France, and to bring Charles VII (1403–1461) to Reims for coronation as French king.

Not surprisingly, as an illiterate, 16-year-old peasant girl from Domrémy, St. Joan's initial attempt to contact the young Dauphin (uncrowned king) was met with sarcastic derision. Nevertheless, after she miraculously predicted the outcome of a military battle before it was officially known, St. Joan was safely escorted through enemy territory to the royal court at Chinon to meet Charles in 1429.

Even though the 17-year-old Joan of Arc made an immediate favorable impression on the 26-year-old Charles, he understandably had to carefully examine her moral character and Christian orthodoxy so as not to be accused of accepting spiritual advice from a heretic or sorceress. A royal commission of inquiry "declared her to be of irreproachable life, a good Christian, possessed of the virtues of humility, honesty and simplicity."

To further test St. Joan's claims that her mission to the king was divinely inspired, she was sent to the besieged city of Orléans to see if she could provide a military victory there as she had divinely predicted. Once at Orléans, many of the noblemen commanding the army accepted and applied St. Joan's military advice believing it to be divinely inspired. While St. Joan herself never fought with a sword, she preferred to carry the army's banner into battle, and was occasionally wounded as a result.

Following months of military failure to repel the English assault on Orléans, with St. Joan's inspiration, advice and leadership, the king's defenders quickly forced the English to retreat. The English, of course, refused to believe that their armies were defeated by a divinely-inspired peasant girl, and concluded she was possessed by the devil.

With the sudden victory at Orléans, as St. Joan had prophesized, she gained the confidence of Charles and his commanders to march on Reims to regain the city. Since Reims was deep within enemy territory, St. Joan and the French forces had to win a number of decisive victories in order to enter Reims; which they did in only two short months. After the army entered the city gates of Reims on 16 July 1429, Charles VII was hastily and officially coronated the very next morning.

Following the coronation, St. Joan's inspired advice was to quickly move to recapture Paris. Unfortunately, her advice was ignored; the royal court preferring to negotiate a truce with Duke Philip of Burgundy, who was allied with the English in the defense of Paris. However, the devious Duke used this phony truce to strengthen and reinforce the Parisian defenses. Consequently, Charles' later assault on Paris was unsuccessful, despite his superior troops.

Shortly afterward, a truce with England was negotiated which lasted only a few months. With the resumption of hostilities, St. Joan traveled to Compiègne to help defend the city against a joint siege by the English and Burgundians. Unfortunately, on 23 May 1430, St. Joan was ambushed, captured and imprisoned by the Burgundians.

While captive in the Beaurevoir Castle, St. Joan made several unsuccessful escape attempts; and was eventually sold to the English who transferred her to Rouen to stand trial. Predictably, the trial was a fraudulent "kangaroo court," whose entire purpose was to permanently rid the English army of a political and military embarrassment.

To accomplish this, a bogus Church tribunal of corrupt Burgundian and pro-English clerics was assembled with the sole intent of proving heresy on the part of St. Joan—a capital offense at that time. Even though there were twelve articles of accusation against St. Joan, the illiterate teenage peasant girl managed to repeatedly avoid the theological entrapments that were deviously designed to provoke a heretical response.

For heresy to be a capital crime, it had to be repeated; so the illegitimate tribunal—desperate for an executable conviction—decided to use "cross-dressing" as St. Joan's repeated heresy. This charge was preposterous, of course, since St. Joan only wore male armour and attire when it was militarily necessary for her own protection. Nevertheless, the sham and shameful trial condemned St. Joan, despite her obvious innocence on all counts; and wickedly sentenced her to death on 30 May 1431.

Even though the Hundred Years' War between France and England continued for another 22 years after St. Joan's martyrdom, the eventual victory of Charles VII as the legitimate king of France and the survival of France as an autonomous European kingdom would not have occurred without the divinely-inspired assistance of Joan of Arc, the "Maid of Orléans."

A further testament to St. Joan's exceptional mission as a divinely-appointed warrior of God is the interesting fact that for generations prior to her birth, there had been various prophecies which indicated that France would "be restored by a virgin" from the "borders of Lorraine"; and "who would work miracles."

Few people today are aware of the fact that the raising up of President Donald J. Trump as an unlikely 21st-century warrior of God was also religiously prophesized well in advance by the "Hermit of Loreto."

4.2   The Prophecy of the Hermit of Loreto

In the early 1980s, a Catholic-American "holy man" living in Italy named Tom Zimmer (1924–2009) is said to have prophetically declared:

> There is a man right now who I believe in the future is going to lead America back to God … the man who in the future is going to lead our country back to God is Donald J. Trump.

Zimmer apparently shared this premonition with an Italian-American psychiatrist named Claudio Curran. Not surprisingly at the time, Dr. Curran is purported to have incredulously replied, "You mean the New York playboy?"

Nevertheless, according to Dr. Curran, Zimmer was so certain of his spiritual premonition that Donald Trump would spiritually transform America in the future that he wrote Trump's name on one of the bricks used in 1984 to seal up the Holy Doors in St. Peter's Basilica at the completion of John Paul II's Jubilee Year. Those bricks remained until the next Jubilee Year in 2000, when they were removed and the

Holy Doors reopened.

It is traditionally regarded that the prayer intentions written on these bricks become part of every Mass conducted in St. Peter's until the bricks are removed for the next Jubilee Year. It was Tom Zimmer's intention, then, for Donald Trump to receive the prayer blessings of all these Masses for his future spiritual mission to America.

So, how credible is Tom Zimmer as a modern-day prophet? Well, by all accounts he was a deeply religious man who put his Catholic faith into quiet action. In the early 1970s, Tom and an American friend, Harry Faulhaber, made a pilgrimage to San Damiano in northwest Italy. This resulted in the two friends co-authoring a little book of prayer called *The Pieta*. While Tom stayed in Italy, Harry returned to America and had the prayer book published. The "Little Blue Prayer Book" (as it became affectionately known) proved to be remarkably popular, and went on to sell millions of copies.

During his time in Italy, Tom spent many years in Rome and authored a second book, this time in Italian, entitled *Sacro Capo di Gesu* ("The Holy Head of Christ"). While in Rome, Tom also got to know Benedict XVI quite well; and since he was fluent in five languages, Tom was able to converse with the German Pope in his native language.

Around 1993, Tom moved to Loreto, Italy, the pilgrimage site of the miraculous House of Mary from Nazareth. According to Catholic tradition, when Muslim invaders threatened to destroy the childhood home of Blessed Mary where the annunciation of Christ's incarnation had taken place, on 10 May 1291 angels miraculously transported the entire house in Nazareth to safety—first to Tersatto, Dalmatia (present-day Croatia); then to Recanati, Italy; and finally to Loreto.

Tom spent fifteen years in Loreto, praying in and around the Holy House of Mary. Some of the Capuchin Franciscan friars who have staffed the basilica of the Holy House since the 1920s, recalled that Tom would often attend four to five Masses a day. Such constant and fervent Catholic devotion eventually earned Tom the title—the "Hermit of Loreto."

Sensing that he didn't have long to live, Tom returned to his American homeland in November 2008; and died about a year later in a Veteran's rest home in Florida on 10 September 2009. Sadly, the Hermit of Loreto was not alive to see his prophecy fulfilled with the presidential election of Donald J. Trump in 2016.

What we know of this prophecy today is courtesy of American priest, Fr. Giacomo Capoverdi. According to Fr. Capoverdi, in a talk he had with Claudio Curran early in 2017, the doctor shared the unusual conversation he had with Tom Zimmer in the early 1980s about the "Trump Prophesy." No doubt the Hermit's prediction seemed so preposterous to Dr. Curran that he made no mention of it until after Trump was elected president.

And even when Fr. Capoverdi was told of Zimmer's prophecy, he in turn said nothing until he heard Melania Trump recite the Lord's Prayer at a Florida rally on 18 February 2017. Fr. Capoverdi was so moved by the rare sight of a Presidential First Lady opening a public rally with a prayer to God that he posted the "Trump Prophesy" on YouTube the very next day (which quickly went viral). Fr. Capoverdi further concludes at the end of the video that in his opinion Zimmer's prophecy is unquestionably authentic:

> This premonition, I firmly believe that Tom Zimmer, this very holy Hermit of Loreto, a promise would happen—has been fulfilled.

4.3 Defending Religious Freedom, Judeo-Christian Culture and Western Civilization

While the prophecy of the Hermit of Loreto certainly

lends weight to the assertion that President Trump has been divinely prepared ("raised up") as an unlikely warrior of God, one can also reasonably come to this conclusion entirely on the basis of his pro-Christian behaviour as US president. As Christ himself declared in Matthew (7:16–20):

> You will know them by their fruits. Are grapes gathered from thorns, or figs from thistles? So, every sound tree bears good fruit, but the bad tree bears evil fruit ... Thus you will know them by their fruits.

President Trump is certainly bearing positive religious fruit in America and abroad. In a little over a year in office, he has already accomplished numerous and significant reforms in an effort to bring America back to God. Some of these accomplishments are listed below:

- He chose Indiana Governor, Mike Pence, a well-respected Christian conservative to be his complementary vice-president.
- He considers female Christian televangelist, Paula White, as a long-time and trusted spiritual advisor. Rev. White, the first female clergy member to pray at a presidential inauguration, has stated that President Trump, has "a heart for God, a hunger for God."
- In a 2017 speech at the 12th annual Values Voter Summit, he stating that he's "stopping cold the attacks on Judeo-Christian values."
- Also at the Summit, he ended Obama's leftist war on Christmas by declaring:

> We're getting near that beautiful Christmas season that people don't talk about any more, they don't use the word Christmas because it is not politically correct ... Well guess what, we're saying Merry Christmas again.

Moreover, in a video conference to the five branches of

the American military, he said several times that he was wishing them a "very, very Merry Christmas," and added, "We say Christmas again very proudly."

- He signed an executive order prohibiting the Internal Revenue Service (IRS) from enforcing the Johnson Amendment, if to do so would directly infringe on an individual's or a corporation's freedom of speech and religion for "speaking out on moral or political issues from a religious perspective."

- Following the end of catastrophic Hurricane Harvey in 2017, he declared a national day of prayer for 3 September.

- In January 2017, he signed an executive order that reinstated the "Mexico City Policy" which prohibits non-governmental organizations (NGOs) that receive U.S. funds—such as the infamous International Planned Parenthood—from providing or promoting overseas abortions; and from advocating for pro-abortion laws in other countries.

- He signed legislation that allows State governments to withhold funds from organizations that perform abortions (particularly Planned Parenthood); thereby rescinding the previous Obama era prohibition.

- He ordered that American funds to the UN not go to the United Nations Population Fund (UNFPA), which is complicit with China's state-enforced "One-Child Policy" that results in forced abortions.

- Under his administration, the US Department of Health and Human Services (HHS) in their "2018–2022 Plan" acknowledges the pro-life assertion that human life begins at conception. In the Introduction it now states:

> HHS accomplishes its mission through programs and initiatives that cover a wide spectrum of activities, serving and protecting Americans at every stage of life, beginning at conception.

Moreover, HHS has also established a new "Conscience and Religious Freedom Division" within the agency's Office for Civil Rights. The new division is responsible for handling "religious freedom complaints" from health care providers. It also aims to protect doctors and other medical professionals who don't want to perform abortions, treat transgender patients or take part in other types of care that is contrary to their religious beliefs.

- In a 2018 letter issued to the Kansas City convention of the National Right to Life Committee, President Trump unequivocally stated:

> We all have a duty to defend the most basic and fundamental human right—the right to life. As President I am dedicated to protecting the lives of every American including the unborn.

- He picked conservative-minded, federal appeals-court judge, Neil Gorsuch, to succeed Antonin Scalia on the United States Supreme Court.

- In 2017, US Vice-President Mike Pence gave a supportive speech at the annual March for Life anti-abortion rally held in Washington, D.C.—the first time for a sitting vice-president to do so. Even more significant in 2018, President Trump himself addressed the pro-life march by satellite communication; once again, a historic first.

- He has been a strong and unwavering supporter and defender of the State of Israel. One courageous example is the recognition of Jerusalem as the undivided capital of Israel by moving the US embassy there from Tel Aviv. Additionally, the US has withdrawn from the UN agency "UNESCO" because of its pronounced anti-Israeli, pro-Palestinian bias. Similarly, the US has also more recently withdrawn from the UN Human Rights Council because of its "relentless, pathological campaign" against Israel. President Trump is also the first sitting US president to visit and pray at the Western Wall, one of the holiest sites in Judaism.

- At the 2017 G20 Summit in Europe, he decisively and courageously defended and promoted Christian, American and traditional Western values (such as God, family, and national sovereignty); unlike Obama's previous socialist position, and the current leftist European leadership.

- In a 2017 speech he gave in Poland, he recounted historical Polish struggles, denounced "radical Islamic terrorism," and sympathetically declared:

> As I stand here today before this incredible crowd, this faithful nation, we can still hear those voices that echo through history. Their message is as true today as ever. The people of Poland, the people of America, and the people of Europe still cry out "We want God."

- Even though the US Constitution clearly prohibits the government from building houses of worship, after the devastation of Hurricane Harvey, the Trump administration permitted FEMA (the Federal Emergency Management Agency) to now use federal money to help rebuild churches damaged by natural disasters.

- Undoing Obama's shameful legacy of ignoring the discrimination and persecution of Christians at home and abroad, President Trump has instructed the State Department to bypass the United Nations and use faith-based organizations to help Iraqi Christians and other persecuted Christian minorities throughout the Middle East.

- The sweeping tax changes that Trump signed into law in late-2017 prompted the chairman of the Faith and Freedom Coalition, Ralph Reed, to declare:

> We have shifted the center of gravity in Republican

fiscal orthodoxy from being something that is purely supply-side and pro-growth—even though I support all that—to a tax code that is pro-child, pro-life and pro-family.

- Prior to his official announcement to run for US president, in a 2015 interview with The Brody File, Trump boldly stated:

  So you tell me about religious liberty and freedom. The Christians are being treated horribly because we have nobody to represent the Christians. Believe me, if I run and I win, I will be the greatest representative of the Christians they've had in a long time.

- When Trump formally announced his campaign for the Republican presidential nomination in 2015, he declared: "I will be the greatest jobs president God ever created, I tell you that." At the time, many regarded this statement as exaggerated bravado. Unbelievably, however, Trump created one million new jobs in his first six months in office; and about three-and-a half million by mid-2018.

- When he took the oath of office on Inauguration Day, his hand rested on the Abraham Lincoln Bible and his family Bible, of which he has said: "My mother gave me this Bible. This very Bible many years ago ... and it's just very special to me." Trump has called the Bible his favorite book, and he referred to it often when he was campaigning for president.

Even though further evidence could easily be listed here to continue demonstrating that Donald Trump as US president is unquestionably a "warrior of God," clearly such is entirely unnecessary. Ironically in fact, even though radical-socialists don't believe in God, they know without question that President Trump is defending and promoting God, Christianity, traditional family values and Western civilization—this, of course, seriously threatens their one-world globalist agenda.

The atheistic-left worldwide is still at a complete loss to understand and explain how a brash, egocentric New York playboy and real-estate developer could become such a powerful existential threat to their longed-for new world order.[48]

4.4 Necessary Qualifications to Overthrow the Elitist Political and Economic Establishments

4.4.1 Trump's Sincere Religious Devotion and Practice Resonates with Mainstream Voters

Prior to his stunning presidential victory, critics of Donald Trump questioned the depth and sincerity of his religious faith. Once in office, any further doubt quickly evaporated. Instead, the atheistic-socialists in America are now frantically concerned that President Trump is too religious, and are fearful that he is "cramming God down their throats."

Thankfully, President Trump is not a hard-line, religious fundamentalist. Religious fundamentalism—whether Hindu, Christian, Islamic or Jewish—is characteristically extremist and fanatical. As such, all forms are unbalanced, unhealthy and harmful. Rather than forcing religion on unwilling Americans, Trump is merely restoring the religious freedoms guaranteed by the First Amendment to the US Constitution. Unfortunately, those freedoms (particularly Christian) were under governmental attack by the socialist agenda of the previous Obama administration.

In Donald Trump's case, he was raised Presbyterian (hardly a radical Christian denomination) and attended Marble Collegiate Church in lower Manhattan, one of the oldest continuous Protestant congregations in North

America. The church minister at that time was Reverend Norman Vincent Peale (1898–1993), the well-known author of the best-selling book, *The Power of Positive Thinking* (1952). No doubt it was the childhood influence of Rev. Peale that largely contributed to Donald Trump's characteristically optimistic attitude towards life and adversity. This deep-seated positivity would serve him well in his spiritual mission as US president; since he is destined to experience more personal attack than any other president in American history.

By self-sacrificially taking on the tremendous burden of US president at this critical time in world history, Donald Trump is knowingly following in the footsteps of Christ-Jesus who took on the burden of world sin in order to provide a path to eternal salvation. The fact that Donald Trump knows the magnitude of his divinely-appointed mission is perhaps best revealed by his forceful words and images in a televised advertisement when he was campaigning for president, entitled, "Donald Trump's Argument for America," in which he stated:

> Our movement is about replacing a failed and corrupt political establishment [*image shown of FBI Director James Comey and Hillary Clinton*] with a new government controlled by you, the American people. The establishment has trillions of dollars at stake in this election. For those who control the levers of power in Washington, [*image of George Soros and Fed Chair Janet Yellen*] and for the global special interests, [*image of G20 leaders*] they partner with these people that don't have your good in mind [*image of Hillary Clinton*].
>
> The political establishment that is trying to stop us [*image of Federal Reserve*] is the same group responsible for our disastrous trade deals [*image of NAFTA and TPP*], massive illegal immigration, and economic and foreign policies that have bled our country dry. The political establishment [*image of Bill and Hillary Clinton*] has brought

about the destruction of our factories and our jobs as they flee to Mexico, China and other countries all around the world. It's a global power structure [*image of G20 and G8*] that is responsible for the economic decisions that have robbed our working class, stripped our country of its wealth, and put that money into the pockets of a handful of large corporations and political entities [*image of Goldman Sachs CEO, Lloyd Blankfein*].

The only thing that can stop this corrupt machine is you. The only force strong enough to save our country is us. The only people brave enough to vote out this corrupt establishment is you, the American people.

I'm doing this for the people and for the movement; and we will take back this country for you, and we will make America great again.

Hillary Clinton and her fellow radical-socialists in America (and abroad) cannot comprehend how a flamboyant New York billionaire, real-estate developer and TV personality with no political experience could become a powerfully-effective US president; a champion of the forgotten American middle-class; and a strong defender of religious freedom, national sovereignty, fair trade and Judeo-Christian values. The ultimate irony is that everything which appears on the surface to make Donald Trump an unlikely candidate for president and an unlikely warrior of God is exactly what has perfectly prepared him for his extraordinary mission as US president.

4.4.2 Being a Multi-Billionaire Frees Trump from Corrupt Establishment Control

For example, the fact that Donald Trump is himself a multi-billionaire is a crucially-necessary qualification to resist and expose the far-too-influential and corrupt big-money donors behind the Democratic and Republican Parties. As a billionaire president, then, Donald Trump is financially free and independent from any lobbyist control, or any undue political pressure from fat-cat party donors; such as George Soros for Democrats, or the Koch brothers for Republicans.[49]

As outlandish as it may appear at first, even Donald Trump's past as a wealthy New York playboy has also provided him with invaluable experience that he critically needs to fulfill his divinely-appointed mission. Having spent a great deal of his adult life in the public eye and under constant media scrutiny, Donald Trump was well-prepared to handle the disproportionate vitriol of the establishment media whose intent is not to report the news, but to destroy him as president. Undoubtedly, most individuals would have mentally and emotionally withered under such pressure and hostility.

In President Trump's case, however, it is obvious that—not only does he remain steadfast and composed—but he actually thrives under the totally-biased media onslaught. Moreover, by fighting back, President Trump has held a public mirror up to the corrupt, leftist media and exposed them for what they have truly become—"fake news." It is thoroughly disturbing for honest, truth-loving citizens to discover that most of the American mainstream media outlets—such as CNN, MSNBC, NBC News, CBS News, ABC News, the Huffington Post, the Washington Post, and the New York Times—are nothing more than propaganda peddlers for the socialist Democratic Party and the radical-left.[50]

As a wealthy New York playboy for much of his early-adult life, Donald Trump obviously needed to be concerned for his personal safety and privacy protection. Unlike most ordinary citizens, and even most politicians, it would be commonplace for him to be accompanied by bodyguard protection, to have his various residences and offices well secured and effectively alarmed, and to make sure that his personal privacy was not compromised by any covert surveillance technology.

As a result of this constant need for precautionary protection for much of his flamboyant adult life, Donald Trump is well used to the high level of security needed to protect him as US president. Once again, ordinary citizens would crumble under the mental and emotional strain of such a life-style; but not Donald Trump. In fact, given the extreme level of Trump-hating rhetoric regurgitated on social media and by the treasonist fake news media, President Trump has most certainly needed an even greater level of Secret Service protection.

It's disturbing to think in a Western democracy today that the one-world socialists are so threatened by President Trump that one of their covert strategies to destroy him is to whip-up frenzied public hysteria over fake news narratives ("Trump Derangement Syndrome") in the treasonist hope that some unhinged leftist lunatic will assassinate the president.[51] We are living in dark spiritual times indeed.

Just as disturbing is the fact that there have been corrupt forces within the Republican establishment which were also threatened by a Donald Trump presidency. In a 2015 interview with MSNBC's Chris Hayes, a Republican establishment consultant named Rick Wilson remarked that because "Trump is still a very powerful force right now," the donor class "can't just sit back on the sidelines and say, 'oh well, don't worry, this will all work itself out.'" According to Wilson, "They're still going to have to go out and put a bullet in Donald Trump, and that's a fact."

4.4.3 Deal-Making Skills as a New York Tycoon Needed to Negotiate with Ruthless World Leaders

Donald Trump's prior experience as a high-powered, real-estate developer uniquely qualifies him to take on the political and economic establishments in America and abroad. Critics have attempted to minimize or dismiss Donald Trump's significant accomplishments as a real-estate developer by dismissively implying that he was "born with a silver spoon in his mouth."

While the young Trump certainly benefited from several trust funds set up by his father Fred and paternal grandmother Elizabeth; and while he certainly had a leg up in the real-estate industry in New York by starting work with his father's successful housing business—he nevertheless didn't squander his inheritance. Instead, when the 25-year-old Trump was promoted to company president in 1971, he renamed the family business "The Trump Organization," and began expanding it from Queens and Brooklyn into Manhattan. Under Trump's bold initiatives, The Trump Organization ventured out from small-scale houses, barracks and apartments into large-scale skyscrapers, hotels, casinos, and golf courses.

So, despite having some initial family assistance—by dint of hard work, risk taking, bold investing, perseverance, toughness and foresight—Donald Trump became a "self-made man." This helps to explain how and why a New York billionaire can easily and honestly relate to regular, hard-working, middle-class Americans; and how and why these same Americans can regard him as their political champion in Washington.

Moreover, the financial and intellectual elites in New York have always looked down their hypocritical noses at "upstart" Donald Trump; considering him boorish, unsophisticated and an unwelcomed outsider. As a result, Trump experientially understands exactly how middle-Americans feel because of the snobbish, disdainful and dismissive treatment of the New York, Washington, Hollywood and Silicon Valley elites.[52]

In order to survive in the combative world of big-league

real-estate development, Trump has remarked that it was absolutely necessary to develop a "killer instinct." This of course is not to say that it was necessary to engage in Mafia-style contract "hits" in order to succeed in business. But rather, in order to negotiate tough business deals, it was crucially necessary to quickly and accurately assess your opponents strengths and weaknesses; to not back down from a difficult fight; to strike back hard when attacked by your opponent; to go directly (not indirectly) for the attacker; to deal from a position of strength;[53] to honestly mean what you say, and not to mislead or bluff your opponent;[54] and to put everything you have into winning a worthwhile fight.

Having a killer instinct when negotiating high-powered business deals and financial negotiations does not mean that Donald Trump is a violent or vengeful person. On the contrary; to any unbiased observer, and as those close to him will readily attest, Trump is also a kind, generous, compassionate, fair-minded, intelligent, hard-working, humourous, friendly and considerate individual.

Trump's carefully-honed combative skills as a tough-minded deal-maker were invaluable in winning the Republican nomination for president. Unfortunately for the other sixteen optimistic candidates, they never knew what hit them. None of these other candidates were able to survive a one-on-one verbal exchange with contender Trump, as he slowly and assiduously dispatched each of them, one by one.

Furthermore, few politicians in the world can match Donald Trump's amazing physical and mental stamina and strength. According to presidential physician Dr. Ronny Jackson who examined President Trump in 2018:

> Based on his cardiac assessment, hands down, there is no question he is in the excellent range ... He has incredibly good genes, and it's just the way God made him ... if he had a healthier diet over the last 20 years he might live to be 200 years old.

But more amazingly, President Trump is one of those rare individuals (about one percent of the population) who thrive on little to no sleep; a condition medically referred to as "short sleeping." According to Dr. Jackson, Trump only sleeps four to five hours a night: "He's just one of those people, I think, that just does not require a lot of sleep."

Other world leaders have quickly discovered that while President Trump can be a powerful, friendly and fair-minded ally, one would be extremely foolish to engage in any one-on-one confrontation with him.[55] Unlike the feckless and conciliatory Barak Obama, President Trump can stand up to ruthless world leaders and dictators such as Vladimir Putin of Russia, Xi Jinping of China, Kim Jong-un of North Korea, Bashar al-Assad of Syria and Ali Khamenei of Iran. Also noteworthy, in less than a year under President Trump, the US military has essentially crushed the ISIS caliphate, recapturing 98 percent of the territory it once controlled.[56]

4.4.4 Experience as a Television Celebrity Developed Necessary Media-Communication Skills

Similar to the fact that Ronald Regan's experience as a Hollywood movie actor greatly contributed to his presidential skill at being "The Great Communicator," Donald Trump's experience on the hit television series, "The Apprentice," undoubtedly helped him develop very effective and necessary media-communication skills as well.

Rather astutely, the British producer of "The Apprentice," Mark Burnett, deliberately chose Donald Trump to star in the hit series because of his brash, larger-than-life personality. As Burnett has described, Trump struck him as:

> [A] real American maverick tycoon … [who] will say whatever he wants … He takes no prisoners. If you're Donald's friend, he'll defend you all day long. If you're not, he's going to "kill you." And that's very American.

He's like the guys who built the West. America is the one country that supports the entire world—because of guys like Donald, who create jobs and a tax base that can support the entire planet.

"The Apprentice" [is] a love letter from me to America, and to New York City; because we chose New York City, about what makes America great.

One very effective and persuasive communication skill that Donald Trump has learned to use over the years is to directly and honestly say what you think to an audience. Conservative, middle-class voters are fed-up with slick, Obama-style rhetoric that is deceptively all-style and no-substance. Moreover, Trump's every-day, non-academic language resonates with ordinary citizens (but not the intellectual elites, of course).

As a result of being direct and "up front" in his communication with others, people know exactly what to expect from Donald Trump, and who he is. It's no secret, then, that Trump was a womanizer in his younger days; that he had sex with a porn star; that he has made crude, off-colour remarks in the past; that he was once a Democrat; that he was previously friends with the Clintons; that Soros helped finance the Trump Hotel in Chicago; that he once supported abortion under certain circumstances; that he has made some unprofitable business decisions; and that he hasn't always been a great husband.

Ordinary, middle-class Americans understand that no one is perfect; that we all have made mistakes in the past; that most people have told crude jokes or made obscene remarks at some point in their lives; that we no longer like some of our previous, "so-called" friends; that we have completely changed some of our once-firm opinions on controversial topics; and that we haven't always been kind to the people around us.

Typically, Christian Americans are especially

understanding of human frailty and weakness since their religious faith teaches them that everyone is a sinner; but that everyone can be divinely forgiven by sincere repentance and reconciliation. Furthermore, many Christian saints are very convincing testaments to the power of true spiritual conversion: St. Augustine (354–430) was previously a dissolute womanizer and profligate; while St. Paul (c.5–c.67) previously executed and imprisoned innocent Christians; and St. Mary of Egypt (c.344–c.421) was a prostitute for over seventeen years; Blessed Bartolo Longo (1841–1926) was previously a Satanic priest; and St. Vladimir (956-1015) murdered his older brother, raped his sister-in-law, had a harem of several hundred women, erected a pagan temple and practiced human sacrifice.

Since atheistic-socialists do not accept or understand Christian concepts such as human sinfulness, divine forgiveness or spiritual conversion, they are much more quick to judge and condemn individuals on the basis of previous indiscretions, even though that particular individual may have completely changed and overcome their past misconduct. To an atheistic-socialist, then, in the case of Donald Trump: "once a womanizer, always a womanizer." If Trump was crude in the past, then he is crude today. If Trump has changed his view on abortion, then he is indecisive or dishonest. If Trump had sex with a porn star in the past, then he must still be cheating on his wife. If he made some unsuccessful business deals in the past, then he must be a poor deal-maker today.

The Trump-hating media has also made a great deal of bogus noise about the president's "so-called" lies and false statements. Of course they are doing so in order to counter President Trump's effective and accurate accusations about their own dishonest and deceptive fake news. Besides, much of what they regard as falsehoods are simply harmless exaggerations that Trump intentionally uses as an effective communicator. In *The Art of the Deal*, he explained this communication technique as follows:

> The final key to the way I promote is bravado. I play to people's fantasies. People may not always think big themselves, but they can still get very excited by those who do. That's why a little hyperbole never hurts. People want to believe that something is the biggest and the greatest and the most spectacular. I call it truthful hyperbole. It's an innocent form of exaggeration—and a very effective form of promotion.

Disreputable and unprofessional psychiatrists have shoddily-diagnosed and publicly proclaimed that Donald Trump's self-acknowledged bravado and hyperbole are instead unhealthy signs of "narcissism" or "egotism" or "megalomania." What these quack physicians clearly don't understand is that for President Trump to confront and overthrow the political and financial elites it is crucially necessary to have an unshakeable sense of self; that is, a securely-centred ego-awareness that can withstand the personal and psychological attacks of powerful enemies. Moreover, because of his spiritual connection to Christ-Jesus—the instiller of divine love—Trump's powerful ego is compassionately united through Christ with his fellow human beings and thereby safeguarded from unhealthy selfishness, egotism and egomania.

President Trump's rock-solid self-confidence, self-assurance and self-reliance were exactly the qualities needed to confront and disarm the corrupt establishment media in America. Unfortunately for the "lamestream" leftist media, they never anticipated, nor were they prepared for, Trump's well-recognized combative nature. Prior to President Trump, unscrupulous media outlets in America had arrogantly assumed the Obama-sanctioned, anti-democratic, socialist role of being the "creators of news" and the "shapers of public opinion," rather than being the unbiased "reporters of news."

Moreover, as the self-appointed manipulators of public opinion, the leftist media were smugly confident that they could successfully brainwash the American voting public to vote for Democrat Hillary Clinton in the 2016 presidential election. Clearly, this was why the Huffington Post publicized a 98.1 percent chance of Hillary winning; CNN declared that Hillary had a 91 percent chance of winning; Reuters/Ipsos predicted a 90 percent chance of Hillary winning; the New York Times gave Hillary an 85 percent chance of winning; and MSNBC reported that Hillary had a 100 percent chance of winning.

Obviously these totally inaccurate media predictions were not the result of poor polling technique; but instead, the deliberate attempt to persuade undecided voters to vote for Hillary Clinton. The logic being, if "crooked Hillary" was virtually certain to win, don't bother wasting a vote on Donald Trump. Unfortunately for the leftist media, they don't have as much persuasive propaganda-power as they arrogantly assume.

Nevertheless, they certainly have huge persuasive influence over the emotionally-driven radical-leftists. Characteristically, since dedicated socialists are mentally driven by group-think, rather than independent logic and reasoning, the propaganda mills of the Trump-hating media easily blow them about like dandelion seeds in the wind. Middle-Americans, however, who haven't been indoctrinated by a university socialist-education, reject and ignore the leftist media outlets. No doubt, this explains why conservative cable-television network, Fox News Channel, has increasingly crushed its leftist competitors MSNBC and CNN throughout the duration of the Trump presidency.[57]

Since the leftist, Democratic-Party-supporting media were unable to sway the presidential election as planned, they have channeled their rejection-anger and fear into a series of sordid attempts at undoing the democratically-elected president —such as calling for impeachment, contriving phony scandals, alleging Russian collusion, publicizing a fictitiously-salacious dossier, questioning his sanity, continually deprecating his exceptional accomplishments, demonizing his character, and verbally attacking his family members. By doing so, the combative President Trump has increasingly drawn the biased media out into the open and exposed their devious machinations and dark manipulations to the light of public awareness.

The media-savvy Trump has also effectively used social media—such as Twitter and Facebook—to circumvent the biased filter of the leftist media; and thereby speak directly to the American public. In fact, his now-famous tweets currently command an international audience: from high-school students to high-powered statesmen. Trump also effectively communicates directly to the American public by speaking at regularly-scheduled, state-wide rallies. Attendees are eagerly captivated by President Trump's relaxed, easy-going, engaging, humourous, animated, entertaining, down-to-earth, and inspiring speaking style.

According to Mark Weinberg, a former speechwriter and advisor to President Ronald Reagan:

> Donald Trump is one of the most effective communicators to ever serve as president. Take it from someone who worked for the man dubbed "The Great Communicator" himself …
>
> It is not a coincidence that the two greatest communicators in recent presidential history came from the entertainment industry. Reagan, like Trump, spent many years in front of the camera, learning lines, hitting cues, and mastering the craft of self-expression. Like everyone in the entertainment world, they paid close attention to ratings, because ratings meant either life or

death for their respective programs. This gave both men the talent of knowing what people wanted to hear, and how to make sure they were listening ...

Trump, too, was a skilled television presenter. But he's also mastered another mode of communication with which Reagan was obviously unfamiliar—social media ...

Donald Trump's tweets earn a great deal of criticism, especially by folks in the media. But the point is often missed: the tweets are very effective. They give Trump an international platform to say whatever he wants to say. And he can change, or some might say manipulate, the global news cycle at will. If Trump doesn't like a storyline in the media, he can with one tweet change the entire narrative. Reagan was a great communicator, but Donald Trump is an even more powerful one.

4.5 "Draining the Swamp" of Deep-State Corruption in Washington, D.C.

4.5.1 Hillary Clinton and the "Dirty Dossier" to Damage Donald Trump

When Donald Trump popularly promised on the presidential campaign trail that he was going to "drain the swamp" in Washington, D.C., most listeners took it to mean that he was going to clean up the dark-money collusion between corrupt politicians and unscrupulous lobby groups. Other than Trump, few suspected the extent to which Barak Obama and Hillary Clinton had covertly corrupted the intelligence community into a cesspool of treasonous nepotism in just eight short years.

Disturbingly, if crooked Hillary had weaseled her way into the White House, it is entirely unlikely that any of this "deep-state" corruption would have risen to the light of public awareness. Analogous to worms rising out of the moist ground when an electric probe is inserted, when Donald Trump was presidentially injected into the centre of the Washington political swamp, he acted as a powerful lightning rod that galvanized the deep-state serpents into action and brought their nefarious writhings to the surface of public awareness.

Journalistic investigations and congressional hearings have uncovered the failed deep-state plot to prevent Donald Trump from ever becoming US president. Prior to the election, crooked Hillary and the dirty-tricks DNC were smugly confident that they had a fool-proof "ace-in-the-hole" in case Donald Trump became too popular—and thereby an electoral threat.

Unbeknownst to the general public, Hillary's law firm in Washington, D.C.—Perkins Coie—was paid about $12 million in "so-called" legal fees by the Clinton campaign and the DNC to collect damaging "dirt" on Donald Trump that could be used to derail his presidential campaign. Whereupon in April 2016, attorney Marc Elias hired Washington-based, private investigative firm—Fusion GPS—for $1.2 million to provide "oppositional research" on Donald Trump. The intent of oppositional research is to gather damaging information on a political opponent or other adversary that could be used to weaken or discredit them.

Later in June 2016, Fusion GPS subcontracted British company—Orbis Business Intelligence—for $168,000 to collect any damaging information that the Russians might have on Trump. As former head of the Russia Desk for the British Secret Service (MI6), company owner—Christopher Steele—supposedly had high-level contacts and sources in Russia to provide him with intelligence information. Between June and December 2016, Steele collected 17 memos of Russian-sourced information, which were eventually compiled into a 35-page dossier, later referred to as the

"Steele dossier."

The first memo that was hand-delivered by courier to Fusion GPS was dated June 20, 2016. Subsequently, in July 2016, Steele mistakenly concluded that the information which he had surreptitiously received from his Russian sources was authentic, and could pose a possible threat to US national security. This prompted him to supply a familiar FBI agent in Rome with a written report of his "explosive" findings. Unfortunately, Steele didn't realize at the time that his Russian "sources" were playing him like a fiddle by supplying him with phony disinformation. Some of this obvious disinformation was absurdly lurid and silly salacious detail concerning Donald Trump during an overnight stay in Moscow.[58]

After receiving Steele's report, the FBI also began paying Steele to continue his dirty digging, but soon backed off when Fusion GPS decided in late-summer 2016 to go public with Steele's "dirty dossier," obviously to damage and discredit the Trump campaign. According to *New Yorker* staff writer Jane Mayer (who personally attended one of the meetings): "these encounters were surely sanctioned in some way by Fusion's client, the Clinton campaign"—that is, by crooked Hillary herself.

Unfortunately for Fusion GPS and the Clinton campaign, no news sources were interested in publicizing the dirty dossier since the questionable information could not be confirmed or verified. However, on 31 October 2016, just one week away from the presidential election, the Soros-funded, leftist online publication—*Mother Jones*—published an article that disclosed some of the dossier's unverified allegations without mentioning ex-spy Steele by name. By then it was too late for the dirty dossier to cause any of Hillary's intended damage to the Trump campaign; and as history well confirms, Donald Trump resoundingly won the US presidency.[59]

4.5.2   The FBI Clinton Email Cover-Up Investigation

In the months immediately prior to the 2016 presidential election, the FBI was not particularly interested in investigating Steele's dirty dossier since the Obama-appointed director and deep-state swamp-rat, James Comey, had a much more important matter to deal with—keeping Hillary Clinton out of jail.

At that crucial time during the election campaign, Comey was charged with investigating Clinton's inappropriate use of a family email server in the basement of her home in Chappaqua, N.Y., for official government communication when she was US Secretary of State. Despite Clinton's specious claims to the contrary, using private messaging system software and a private server—rather than official State Department email accounts maintained on secure federal servers—clearly violated State Department protocols and procedures, as well as federal laws and regulations governing recordkeeping.

Moreover, crooked Hillary also falsely maintained that none of the government email content exchanged on her private server was "classified." In fact, Comey himself identified 110 emails as containing information that was classified at the time it was sent—including 65 emails that were "Secret" and 22 that were "Top Secret." Moreover, 2100 emails were also later deemed by the State Department to be classified. Though none of these emails had classification markings, Hillary's non-disclosure agreement stipulated that unmarked classified information should be treated exactly the same as marked classified information.

Even though Secretary Clinton was warned by State Department security personnel that using her own unsecured Blackberry phone for government communication was vulnerability to hacking; and even though the Bureau of Diplomatic Security had also warned her about the danger of being hacked, she continued to use unsecured communication devices despite her knowledge of the surveillance dangers.

Clinton aides and legal advisors later compounded her email criminality after she was served on 4 March 2015, with a congressional subpoena from the House Select Committee on Benghazi, instructing her to turn over her private server and all her emails. Before complying with the subpoena, a Clinton employee deleted over 30,000 emails that were dubiously claimed to be "personal" and "private"; and then completely erased the server's hard-drive with a removal program called BleachBit. Moreover, a State Department aide named Justin Cooper admitted to smashing Clinton's Blackberry cell phones with a hammer; thereby further destroying email evidence required by subpoena (clearly obstruction of justice).

While there was ample evidence that Hillary Clinton and her lackeys contravened numerous laws and government protocols, deep-state Comey had already started drafting a statement exonerating crooked Hillary in late-April to early-May 2016—before interviewing any key witnesses, including Clinton herself. Not surprisingly, then, Comey publically announced in July 2016 that the FBI investigation had concluded that:

> Although there is evidence of potential violations of the statutes regarding the handling of classified information … [and though it was] possible that hostile actors gained access [to her emails] …

then-Secretary Clinton was simply "extremely careless"; and that his recommendation was to not file charges against her.

In whitewashing the FBI investigation into Clinton's unsecured emails, deep-state Comey was assisted by an equally-corrupt, Trump-hating, FBI swamp-rat named Peter Strzok. Strzok was the number-two official in the counterintelligence division who led the Clinton pseudo-investigation. Moreover, it was Strzok who changed Comey's earlier draft language describing Hillary's actions as "grossly negligent" to "extremely careless." This of course was done deliberately so that crooked Hillary would avoid any further legal implications; since the federal law governing the mishandling of classified material establishes criminal penalties for "gross negligence," but not for "extreme carelessness."

Even then-Attorney General Loretta Lynch—as another sordid layer of the Obama deep-state corruption in Washington—attempted to minimize and dismiss the Clinton email scandal by suggesting to Comey that he describe the intelligence agency's work as an FBI "matter," rather than an FBI "criminal investigation." Furthermore, even though Comey had no authority to recommend that no charges be laid against Hillary, then-AG Lynch was happy to comply and announced on 6 July 2016 that no charges would be filed.

Even though FBI Comey exonerated Hillary in July 2016, he later informed Congress on 28 October 2016 that the FBI had acquired further Clinton emails from the laptop of disgraced Congressman Anthony Wiener that required further criminal investigation. By commenting on an FBI investigation so close to a presidential election, Comey was deliberately ignoring the advice of Justice Department officials in a clear effort to cover his own professional butt and avoid any accusations of withholding sensitive information. While crooked Comey was to a point a deep-state Clinton loyalist, he was first and foremost the Machiavellian protector of his own overinflated pseudo-reputation.

While Hillary Clinton has blamed Comey's "October surprise" for her embarrassing election loss, the fact is FBI swamp-rats—Comey, Strzok and other rogue agents—actually kept her out of jail (so far). Since all the deep-state operatives were smugly confident of a Clinton presidential coronation, any FBI announcement of a renewed email investigation close to the election would supposedly have had no negative effect on the American voting public.

The level of deep-state corruption involved in the FBI Clinton email cover-up was readily apparent to any unbiased Republican in government at the time; as echoed in a statement by Republican House leader Paul Ryan:

> These documents demonstrate Hillary Clinton's reckless and downright dangerous handling of classified information during her tenure as secretary of state. They also cast further doubt on the Justice Department's decision to avoid prosecuting what is a clear violation of the law.

4.5.3   Russian Collusion as a Desperate, Deep-State Attempt to Impeach President Trump

Since crooked Hillary's oppositional research firm, Fusion GPS, was unable to galvanize the leftist American media to collectively publish Steele's dirty dossier—in order to damage Trump's reputation and thereby prevent him from being elected president—after Clinton's ignominious defeat, an alternative use for the dirty dossier was concocted; this time to scandalize and impeach newly-elected President Trump. The corrupt, post-election Clinton strategy was to deliver the dirty dossier to the FBI from "seemingly" multiple sources in an effort to pressure the FBI into conducting a criminal investigation that would lead to criminal charges by the US Attorney General's Department.

The first source was former British spy Christopher Steele—the compiler of the dirty dossier—who had already given some of his bogus Russian intel to an FBI agent in Rome in late-summer 2016. A second FBI source was *Mother Jones* reporter David Corn, who received the dirty dossier from Steele because he wanted it published. A third source to deliver the dirty dossier to the FBI was Glenn Simpson himself—the co-founder of Fusion GPS and Steele's boss. A fourth source was Bruce Ohr, an associate deputy attorney general under Obama. Incestuously, Ohr's wife Nellie had been hired by Fusion GPS in 2016 to help find any compromising dirt on then-candidate Donald Trump. Bruce Ohr had met with ex-spy Steele before the presidential election, and with Glenn Simpson after the election (which he originally falsely denied). No doubt Ohr had acquired his copy of the dirty dossier from Glenn Simpson or his wife.

A fifth source was Republican Senator John McCain (1936–2018). As a notorious Washington swamp-rat and avowed Trump-hater, McCain[60] was more than willing to perform his "patriotic duty" of delivering a copy of his secretly-obtained dossier to FBI Director Comey in early-December 2016. McCain had clandestinely received his copy from Sir Andrew Wood (a former British ambassador to Moscow) at a security conference in Canada shortly after the US election. The dirty dossier had been given to Wood by ex-spy Christopher Steele, who had instructed Wood to deliver it to McCain; no doubt in order to give the anti-Trump Russian intel some "congressional weight" with the FBI. McCain also surreptitiously passed a copy to leftist website, *Buzzfeed,* which published the full unverified dossier in January 2017.

So, even though the FBI had received multiple copies of the dirty dossier, it was all coming from Fusion GPS (and employee Steele); who were ultimately under instruction from crooked Hillary herself. Moreover, it is clear that the FBI had determined early-on that much of the dirty dossier was bogus and unreliable. As evidence, FBI Director Comey testified to the Senate Intelligence Committee in June 2017 that the Steele dossier "material" was "salacious and unverified."

Even though the corrupt officials at the FBI—such as Comey and Strzok—knew that they couldn't use the unverified dirty dossier as a pretense for an FBI criminal investigation to discredit then-candidate Trump in 2016, they decided instead to covertly use it as a phony reason to indirectly spy on Trump, with the desperate hope of finding some damaging information on him.

To accomplish this corrupt and nefarious scheme, in October 2016, FBI swamp-rat Peter Strzok used the dirty dossier to obtain a special warrant from the US Foreign Intelligence Surveillance Court (FISC, also called the "FISA Court") to spy on a Trump campaign advisor named Carter Page. The Court was deceptively led to believe that the FBI needed to monitor Page's communications to investigate whether Trump campaign associates (and Trump himself) had colluded with Russian officials to affect the presidential election.

The corrupt FBI anti-Trumpers needed a special FISA warrant to spy on Page because he was an American citizen (and not a foreign agent). But what the FISA Court judges were not explicitly told by the FBI was that the Steele dossier that was used to obtain the warrant had been financed by Hillary Clinton and the DNC as bogus oppositional intel on Donald Trump. The Page surveillance warrant was good for only 90 days, and was consequently renewed three more times after Trump took office).

The false narrative, then, that Donald Trump and/or his associates secretly colluded with Russian officials to rig the presidential election was nefariously hatched by corrupt Clinton loyalists and Obama deep-state swamp-rats in an effort to de-legitimize candidate Trump, and then later President Trump. The leftist mainstream media was of course ready, eager and willing to sacrifice truthful news-casting in order to promote and propagandize this entirely false narrative against President Trump.

Unfortunately for FBI Director Comey, soon after the presidential election he became the subject of a review by the

Trump Justice Department concerning his controversial conduct before and after the Clinton email "investigation." Newly-confirmed Deputy AG Rod Rosenstein (the fellow swamp-rat who renewed the FISA warrant to indirectly spy on Trump)) was forced to conclude that Comey's serious mishandling of the case rendered him unfit for the position of FBI director. As a result, AG Jeff Sessions recommended Comey's removal to then-president Trump, who "hereby terminated and removed [Comey] from office, effective immediately" (on 9 May 2017).

Disgraced Director Comey, however, didn't go quietly. On his way out the Bureau door, Comey had one last dirty trick up his grubby FBI sleeves. He illegally walked out the door with FBI documents (Comey euphemistically called them "personally-written memos") which falsely suggested that President Trump was pressuring him to end the FBI investigation into Russian interference of US elections.

Comey immediately and illicitly leaked these contrived documents to a close friend, Columbia Law School professor Daniel C. Richman; and instructed him to share the contents with a reporter from the *New York Times*, which then published the leaked material on 16 May 2017. Comey openly admitted to a Senate Intelligence Committee hearing in June 2017 that he did this "because I thought that might prompt the appointment of a special counsel."

Comey didn't have to wait long for his devious plan to take effect. On 17 May 2017—only one day after his leaked FBI documents were published—Deputy AG Rod Rosenstein appointed a Justice Department special counsel to investigate:

> any links and/or coordination between the Russian government and individuals associated with the campaign of President Donald Trump, and any matters that arose or may arise directly from the investigation.

Moreover, swamp-rat Rosenstein chose Comey's close

friend, former FBI Director Robert Mueller, to head up the investigation. Mueller in turn assembled a highly-partisan investigative team—of the 17 prosecutors involved: 14 are Democrats, 3 are party unaffiliated, none are Republican. Moreover, a review of Federal Election Commission records shows that 12 investigators donated money to the Democratic Party, with most giving money to either Barack Obama or Hillary Clinton.

Since the ludicrous notion that Donald Trump colluded with the Russians in order to win the US presidency is a fake narrative devised by Clinton loyalists and Obama deep-state hold-overs, the Mueller special counsel investigation is nothing more than a bogus "witch-hunt"; desperately groveling for some compromising piece of dirt, or for some covert way of entrapment (such as perjury), in order to damage and impeach President Trump.

Furthermore, in an effort to assist the Mueller dirt-collection team, DOJ Rosenstein renewed the FISA warrant for a third (and final) time so that Mueller could continue to spy on President Trump and his associates. Not surprisingly, at the time of this writing, Mueller and his Democratic hit-squad have been entirely unsuccessful at damaging President Trump; in fact, their partisan inquisition is more likely to blow up in their own duplicitous faces as time goes by.

It should also be noted that deep-state corruption at that time was not limited to the FBI and the DOJ. The CIA under Director John Brennan, and the DNI (Department of National Intelligence) under Director James Clapper were also corrupted and weaponized during the Obama years. It was swamp-rat Clapper, for example, who originally incited the rabid, left-wing media coverage of a Trump-Russia collusion by leaking to CNN the classified briefings given to then President-elect Donald Trump and President Barack Obama on the dirty dossier. It was only after CNN reported Clapper's briefing leak that *Buzzfeed* decided to publish the entire 35-page dirty dossier.

As for CIA swamp-rat Brennan (who was a communist supporter during the late-1970s and an Islamic convert during the 1990s), it is investigatively concluded that "John Brennan did more than anyone to promulgate the dirty dossier ... He politicized and effectively weaponized what was false intelligence against Trump." As related by Roger Stone in the online article, "John Brennan is the Hoaxmaster General—Did the CIA Play a Part in the Russian Hoax?":

> Brennan did this by systematically and purposefully disseminating the defamatory contents of the sleazy, Clinton-purchased "dirty dossier" to official Washington and numerous sympathetic media mouthpieces during the transition period and beyond, ensuring their continued proliferation, compounding the damage Brennan hoped and expected would result from his calculated treachery.

While there are numerous other Washington swamp-rats that have come to light since Donald Trump became US president and that could be further exposed here, the point is that the general public would have known absolutely nothing of this pervasive and pernicious deep-state corruption if Hillary Clinton had been elected instead. The level of covert corruption would have continued unabatedly to the eventual disintegration and downfall of the entire American Republic.

While a great many swamp-rats have already been exposed, dismissed, removed and fired in the less than two years since Trump took office, few have yet to be criminally charged for their illegal and subversive malfeasance. Moreover, there are still a great many powerful, deep-state denizens lurking in the depths of the Washington swamp that intend to destroy Donald Trump and his divinely-appointed mission to "Make America Great Again."

4.6 "Making America Great Again" is Not About World Domination

In the past when American presidents publicly championed "American greatness," a collective shiver of trepidation ran through the world body-politic. This was a conditioned response from historical experience, since "American greatness" almost always meant "increased American hegemony and imperialism": the political, economic, and military predominance and control of America over other world nations.

It is quite understandable, then, that many government leaders—at home and abroad—would be nervous and concerned with Donald Trump's campaign slogan: "Make America Great Again." Furthermore, his immediate actions as president would appear to suggest a continuing policy of American hegemony: increased military spending; increased use of tariffs on trading partners; the cancellation of multinational trade agreements; tougher immigration enforcement; and increased sanctions against Russia, China, Iran and North Korea.

But in President Trump's case, these decidedly pro-American actions can be deceiving. In the same way that an individual must themself be strong and healthy in order to help others, President Trump fully understands that America must be strong and healthy (economically, militarily, politically and socially) in order to assist other struggling world-nations; and to take a leadership role in striving for global peace, security and stability.

National greatness, however, flies in the face of socialist ideology which promotes a distorted version of "equality" that is contrary to human nature; and therefore contrary to human society. Instead of properly and exclusively applying the principle of equality to the formulation, application and enforcement of government legislation (that is, state law), socialism mistakenly imposes a stricture of equality on everything—on a nation's individual and collective wealth; on personal and national accomplishments; on a nation's culture and ethnicity; on a nation's religious beliefs; on a nation's unique identity; and on a nation's relationship with other countries. All must be "equalized," according to socialist ideology, so that all so-called "victimized" minorities are treated "fairly."

In its ideological obsession to impose an artificial "equality" on all aspects of society, socialism ignores the physical and psychological fact of human nature—individual human beings are inherently "unequal." Human beings differ in height, weight, body-type, skin color, hair colour, eye colour, health, fitness, strength, endurance, facial features, fingerprints, DNA, sex, talents, abilities, intellect, language, attitudes, values, ethics, likes, dislikes, emotions, thoughts, worldview, friends, family, education and experience—just to name a few natural inequalities.

Socialism endeavours to crush individual "uniqueness" in favour of group "collectivism." In other words, the anti-human socialist ideal is to suppress natural personal differences, and to artificially mold individual citizens into selfsame, equally-mechanized cogs in the socialist state-machine. The socialist ruling-elite of course retain their unequal, inordinate wealth, and exempt themselves from any other forced equalizations as well).

Just as radical-socialism assiduously suppresses uniqueness on an individual level, it also fervently criticizes and curtails any patriotic attempts to acknowledge and celebrate any special uniqueness on a national level. What is termed "American exceptionalism" has been historically denounced by the political-left. Just as individual citizens are expected to subsume personal uniqueness in favour of collectivistic equalization, so nation-states are expected to subsume national exceptionalism in favour of the collective, international socialist world-order.

The distorted, international socialist agenda is to transform every nation on earth into a carbon-copy, homogeneous mixture of ethnicity, religion, gender, income level, education, social status and age group. This explains why radical-socialists in America are determined to destroy the country's white-European cultural majority with unrestricted Hispanic immigration from Mexico, Central and South America. Likewise, unrestricted immigration of Middle-Eastern Muslims is intended to destroy America's Christian religious majority as well.

Socialists in America (which now includes the Democratic Party) are also intent on destroying the nation's capitalist economy (thereby preventing the unequal acquisition of personal wealth) through autocratic federal government regulation and onerous taxation. Promoting and legislating homosexual "rights" is socialistically intended to artificially "balance" the cultural predominance of the vast majority of heterosexual men and women in Western society. Free university, free healthcare and guaranteed income are socialist "carrots" intended to give America's naïve youth the false promise of more social status and political power over the predominantly more affluent and privileged elderly class (which has properly earned that position).

Social engineering multi-billionaires, such as George Soros, openly contend that a strong, vibrant and healthy America is a serious impediment to establishing an international socialist order. As a result, they are spending millions of dollars in a colluded covert offensive to prevent President Trump from "Making America Great Again." Under the socialist-style Obama administration, US foreign policy was one of appeasement and apology. By continually granting political and economic concessions to hostile nations such as China, Russia, North Korea and Iran in order to avoid any possible conflict, Obama drastically and purposely weakened the United States as a global superpower; thereby allowing communist China to illicitly, deceptively and dangerously become a rival international power—with the clear intent of overtaking the US in the very near future. Most importantly, whether consciously or intuitively, President Trump understands that the most important component in making America "great" again, is to make America "good" again. As the French philosopher and diplomat Alexis De Tocqueville (1805–1859) wisely stated after observing US churches "aflame with righteousness" that:

America is great because America is good, and if America ever ceases to be good, America will cease to be great.

And this is the primary reason why President Trump is bringing America back to God (as prophesized by the Hermit of Loreto in Chapter subsection 4.2). By reaffirming and defending religious freedom in America, President Trump is re-strengthening the Judeo-Christian ideas, beliefs, values, ethics and lifestyle that made the American breakaway-European colony prosperous and great in the first place.

CHAPTER 5

THE UNDERLYING SPIRITUAL BATTLE TO CONTROL MANKIND

5.1 Lucifer's Age-Old Plan to Control the World

UNFORTUNATELY, MATERIALISTS, secularists and empiricists—by restricting their understanding of reality exclusively to the sense-perceptible dimension of physical matter and energy—fail to acknowledge and understand the underlying dimension of spiritual existence. In fact, the spiritual dimension is the actual causative agent of all activity and occurrence in the physical world. Analogous to invisible energy causing visible matter to move, invisible spiritual forces are the underlying cause of all visible activities in the physical world.

As all the major world religions have historically attested, the invisible spiritual world is not simply comprised of spiritual substances and spiritual forces, it is also home to a myriad of superphysical beings: angels, archangels, seraphim and cherubim to name a few. Moreover, these spiritual beings are understood to be involved in numerous ways with human affairs; some beneficially, others inimically. In Western theology, for instance, St. Michael is known to be a powerful, benevolent archangel who is responsible for the protection of the entire nation of Israel.

Lucifer, on the other hand, is also understood to be a highly-advanced spiritual being; but who fell from his lofty estate through selfish pride and arrogance—thereby becoming a malevolent being opposed to divinely-guided human evolution. Moreover, Lucifer is also biblically understood to be the metaphorical "serpent in paradise" who seductively enticed the primordial ancestors of mankind to willfully disobey the beneficent commandments of God.

This luciferically-inspired "original sin" resulted in a devastating, generational separation of humanity from God; which caused the subsequent negative effects of sickness, disease, debilitation and death. Not only did Lucifer lead mankind astray in ancient times, but he enticed numerous angel-beings to disobey the will of God as well. According to the biblical account, then, Lucifer was the original, archetypical rebel—inspiring and instigating cosmic revolution in heaven and on earth.[61]

The revolutionary ideology of radical-socialism and Marxist-communism did not originate in the human brain; but was subtly and covertly planted there throughout the ages by Lucifer and his renegade angels. Though the constant bombardment of false-news propaganda by the biased media is certainly a powerful factor in programming socialist group-think, group-hatred and group-violence; the currently-widespread, leftist insanity known as "Trump Derangement Syndrome" is best explained by invisible, spiritual forces—that is, by the subconscious, thought-control seduction of luciferic-beings.

As militarily confirmed by brainwashing techniques, when waking consciousness is precariously dampened through fatigue, drugs, alcohol or injury the weakened brain is much more susceptible to foreign hypnotic-suggestion and mind-control. Especially with naïve and unwary young adults, compromised consciousness through pervasive drug and alcohol abuse dangerously increases their subconscious impressionability to socialist media propaganda and to socialist educational indoctrination.

Furthermore, it is clear that the current ideological battle raging between Marxist-socialism and capitalist-democracy throughout Western society (and not just in America) is more than just a cultural war. The fact that radical-socialism and hard-line communism are not just inimical to religion in general; but that they intend to destroy Christianity in particular, seriously expands this societal conflict into being spiritual warfare as well.

As the spiritual instigator of anti-Christian, Marxist ideology, Lucifer and his rebel angels have declared themselves the sworn enemies of Christ-Jesus, the spiritual founder of Christianity. While the mission of Christ-Jesus is to lead humanity back to an increasingly loving relationship with our Father-God, Lucifer's evil-intention is to continually separate humanity from our true home in God; and instead to establish a godless, secularized, socialist world-order in order to siphon off dispirited human beings into an illusionary, superphysical, luciferic earth-realm.

5.2   The Destined Incarnation of the Antichrist[62]

5.2.1   Lucifer and Satan are Two Distinct Supernatural Beings

Even though proud Lucifer may be credited with being the original revolutionary against the divine cosmic order, there are other powerful and malevolent spiritual beings who also disobey the will of God, and who also strive to thwart the true destiny of mankind on earth for their own personal agenda. The Bible mentions a number of perfidious supernatural beings (who were often worshipped as pagan deities); such as: Baal, Moloch, Astarte, Dagon, Abaddon, Beelzebub, Belial, Chemosh, Legion, Adrammelech, Bel, Mammon, Tartak, Nibhaz, Anammelech, Nergal, Ashtaroth and Nisroch. But the greatest amongst this pantheon of false deities and fallen spirits is the being known biblically as Satan.

In Western theology, Satan and Lucifer are often regarded as the same being—with the explanation that "Lucifer" (Latin for "Light-Bearer") was his illustrious name before his ignominious plummet from heavenly grace; and "Satan" (Hebrew for "Adversary") was his name after his dark descent into hell. Esoteric Christianity, however—particularly the spiritual-scientific research of Austrian philosopher and esotericist Rudolf Steiner[63] (1861–1925)—provides ample information on the profound differences between these two renegade spirits.

According to esoteric understanding, Satan (and not Lucifer) is alternatively known by a number of familiar names—such as the devil and Mephistopheles; as well as a number of biblical titles and descriptions, such as: the "prince of demons," the "prince of the power of the air," the "prince of this world," the "father of lies," the "lawless one," the "beast rising out of the sea," and the "great red dragon." An increasing number of Christians today also believe that the "antichrist" mentioned in the Johannine epistles is also a specific reference to Satan.

5.2.2 The Antichrist is a Biblical Reference to Satan (not Lucifer)

Since biblical mention of the Antichrist is rather vague and unspecific, numerous conjectures have sprung up throughout the centuries as to who or what is the Antichrist. Speculations have ranged from the Antichrist being a generalized hostile attitude or demeanor towards Christianity; to the Antichrist being an actual historic figure, such as Nero, or Hitler, or the Pope—or even President Trump!

The general and historical position of Catholic teaching has been to de-emphasize the personal nature of the Antichrist, as evidenced in paragraph 675 of the *Catechism of the Catholic Church*:

> The supreme religious deception is that of the Antichrist, a pseudo-messianism by which man glorifies himself in place of God and of his Messiah come in the flesh.

Nevertheless, there have been prominent Catholic leaders who have maintained that the Antichrist will be the future incarnation of an actual person. Well-known and well-respected archbishop, Venerable Fulton J. Sheen (1895–1979), for example, was very specific about the Antichrist; as in the following quotation from his book, *Communism and the Conscience of the West* (1948):

> The Antichrist will not be so called; otherwise he would have no followers. He will not wear red tights, nor vomit sulphur, nor carry a trident nor wave an arrowed tail as Mephistopheles in *Faust*. This masquerade has helped the Devil convince men that he does not exist.
>
> [H]e will come disguised as the Great Humanitarian; he will talk peace, prosperity and plenty not as means to lead us to God, but as ends in themselves ...
>
> He will tempt Christians with the same three temptations with which he tempted Christ ...
>
> [H]e will have one great secret which he will tell to no one: he will not believe in God. Because his religion will be brotherhood without the fatherhood of God, he will deceive even the elect. He will set up a counterchurch ... It will have all the notes and characteristics of the Church, but in reverse and emptied of its divine content. It will be

a mystical body of the Antichrist that will in all externals resemble the mystical body of Christ.

Once again, even though it's not the official teaching of the Catholic Church, Archbishop Sheen clearly equates the Antichrist with Mephistopheles (undisguised), with the devil and with Satan (the tempter in the wilderness). Associating the Antichrist with Satan has also become currently popular in Christian fundamentalist writings; such as the *Left Behind* series of 38 books by Tim LaHaye, Neesa Hart, Aaron Austin, Michael Standaert, Mark Hitchcock, D.E. Stevenson, Robert Rite, Judith Krantz and Jerry B. Jenkins.

Unfortunately, to atheists, secularists, materialists and empiricists the whole notion of a spiritual world populated with spiritual beings who affect the earth, human society and individual behaviour (both positively and negatively) is regarded as preposterous and absurd—even an indication of an unsound mind. But as Archbishop Sheen alarmingly indicated in the previous quotation on page 139, modern-day ignorance, disbelief and unawareness of spiritual reality has enabled powerfully-malicious supernatural beings to effectively corrupt human behaviour almost entirely unnoticed, and without opposition, by many people living today.

Moreover, even to devout Christians of different denominations, the biblical indication that the devil himself—Satan—is destined to physically incarnate as a human being in the near future is shockingly difficult to comprehend and to accept. One particular reason for disbelief is the common religious understanding that highly-advanced supernatural beings, such as angels and archangels, do not require material bodies to exist; and hence do not physically incarnate. Another reason is that supernatural beings are distinct and more advanced than human beings; and hence would not incarnate in an inferior (to them) human body. This would be analogous to a human being choosing to incarnate in an animal body.

Nevertheless, there are a number of biblical instances where superphysical angels have appeared as physical persons; such as the angel "man" who wrestled with Jacob; the angel "men" who appeared to Abraham and Lot; and the angel "people" who appeared to Joshua, Manoah, Ezekiel, Daniel and Zechariah. Also noteworthy, after his glorious resurrection Christ-Jesus demonstrated that he could appear physically substantial enough to actually consume some fish, and to be tangibly touched by doubting Thomas; and then to physically disappear again.

While it seems to be highly unusual, then, for supernatural beings to appear physically as human beings, according to biblical accounts this has actually occurred a number of times throughout history. Nevertheless, these accounts strongly suggest that these angelic physical appearances were brief and temporary; somewhat similar to Christ-Jesus fleetingly appearing and disappearing in his resurrected body. It's nowhere implied that these angel "men" were born as angel "babies," who then grew up as angel "children" before becoming angel "adults."

In speculating about a possible human incarnation of Satan as the Antichrist, then, it's not entirely clear how this will occur. While one traditional theory suggests that Satan will be born naturally as a human child with extraordinary abilities that will manifest later in adulthood as the Antichrist; the more widely-accepted theory is that Satan will completely "possess" the mind and body of a willing and compliant human adult later in life, and thereby manifest as the Antichrist.

5.2.3 The Infernal Agenda and Current Influence of the Antichrist

It's important to understand at this point that detailed

knowledge and information about the being, nature and evil-intentions of Satan, and his destined human incarnation as the Antichrist, is essential in truly comprehending much of the confusing social upheaval that has engulfed the entire modern world. Unfortunately, because Christian fundamentalist writers have successfully sensationalized and marketed the biblical Antichrist as part of their hyperbolic and fictitious "end-times" world-scenario, the general public now associates any mention of the Antichrist with their radical religious extremism. Consequently, any serious discussion of the Antichrist by non-fundamentalist writers (such as the author of this publication) will often be denigrated, disregarded and very often dismissed.

Nevertheless, it is critically important in the spiritual battle taking place today that sensible, reliable and trustworthy information about the Antichrist be increasingly made available to an unprepared, uninformed and unsuspecting world population. Needless to say, in order to better understand the Antichrist, it is necessary to better understand Satan. Nowhere is there more detailed, more comprehensive, more penetrating, or more transcendent information about the supernatural being known as Satan than in the anthroposophical literature of Rudolf Steiner.

As a highly-respected esotericist and Rosicrucian initiate, Steiner used his prodigious powers of supersensible perception (clairvoyance) to investigate the supernatural world in a precise and rigorous spiritually-scientific way. By conveying his spiritual observations and discoveries in clear intellectual concepts, Steiner was able to share his research with other clairvoyant—and non-clairvoyant—investigators.

Regarding the being of Satan, Steiner preferred to call him "Ahriman," the name for the ancient Persian spirit of darkness. This choice was primarily to avoid all the mythology, folklore, legendary tales and exaggerated misinformation that continues to surround and obfuscate our understanding of Satan as the devil. Most importantly, for example, is the recognition that Satan-Ahriman is not the same being as Lucifer. As a separate supernatural being at an entirely different level of evolutionary development, Ahriman has his own evil-agenda and operates quite differently than Lucifer. For instance, Lucifer (as previously noted) secretly and seductively operates primarily in the realm of human emotion; thereby inciting and stimulating fiery feelings of egotism, self-centred pride, rebellion and revolution. Lucifer's covert and clandestine influence finds outward expression in radical-socialism, hard-line communism and violent social-protest movements.

Ahriman, on the other hand, stealthily and calculatingly operates primarily in the realm of human intellect; thereby implanting cold, dispassionate thoughts and ideas of atheism, materialism, mechanization and empiricism. Where Lucifer fervently desires to *replace* God with himself in future human evolution; Ahriman dispassionately strives to *abolish* God entirely from human conscious-awareness. Ahriman's coldhearted and bloodless influence finds outward expression in secular movements, technological invention and materialistic science.

While Lucifer and Ahriman are adversarial in many significant respects, in certain historical instances they have decided to join forces in order to accomplish a shared nefarious goal. For example, both evil-spirits have set their malevolent sights on human evolution and on planet earth. Both intend on usurping the divinely-intended plan for human evolution; and thereby control the entire planet for themselves. In order to accomplish this godless undertaking, the forces of Lucifer and Ahriman would have to defeat the divinely-appointed protectors of mankind and the earth—Christ and his celestial legions of light.

In the worldwide social upheaval of today, cooperation between Lucifer and Ahriman can be readily observed. The radical-socialism that is insidiously creeping across Western society[63] is a coordinated, diabolic effort between Lucifer and Ahriman: Lucifer is providing the fiery revolutionary fervour that fuels the movement; while Ahriman intellectually underpins the movement with cold, godless Marxist ideology. Their shared goal is the establishment of a socialist-style new world order.

Once that has been achieved, it is agreed that Ahriman—in his human incarnation as the Antichrist—will then become the world-leader of this socialist new world order. Under his control, those human beings who decide to remain on the earth will be offered a form of physical immortality through advanced technology (such as robotics, artificial intelligence, computerization and engineered organ harvesting). Those disillusioned human beings who reject ahrimanic immortality on earth will be illicitly siphoned off after death into a bogus, pseudo-heavenly realm surrounding the earth—created and controlled by Lucifer. Unlike Ahriman, Lucifer abhors physical materiality, and is quite content to confine his own specific rulership of the earth and mankind to a superphysical sphere surrounding the planet.

In this way, then, Lucifer and Ahriman, even though they are characteristically adversarial, jointly plan on carving up the spoils of war—mankind and the earth—between the two of them. Thankfully for God-loving human beings, in order for Lucifer and Ahriman to realize their iniquitous goal, they will have to defeat the powerful divine forces of Christ and the celestial protectors of mankind and the earth.

5.3   The Forces of St. Michael and the Battle Against the Dragon of Materialism

Even 2000 years ago, St. Paul fully understood that behind the outward scenes of human events there was a raging spiritual battle taking place that was reflected in the soul of everyone on earth. He also understood that because this was a supernatural "battle of the gods" which nascent humanity was involuntarily drawn into, human participants were entirely outmatched by powerful supernatural adversaries; and therefore had no chance of succeeding unassisted and alone. As St. Paul eloquently described in Ephesians (6:11, 12):

> Put on the whole armor of God, that you may be able to stand against the wiles of the devil. For we are not contending against flesh and blood, but against the principalities, against the powers, against the world rulers of this present darkness, against the spiritual hosts of wickedness in the heavenly places.

Since the allied spiritual forces of Christ are the most powerful impediment to the continuing evil machinations of Ahriman, the spirit of darkness considers Christ-Jesus his foremost sworn enemy; and is therefore quite happy to be referred to as the "Antichrist." Since Christ-Jesus is much more advanced in evolutionary development than the fallen-spirit Ahriman, he is more than capable of dealing directly with his evil adversary.

Nevertheless, it has been Christ's faithful and mighty warrior, St. Michael the archangel, who has waged spiritual battle with Ahriman throughout the ages. While there have been several of these supernatural skirmishes between these two opposing spirits—known as "wars in heaven"—St. Michael has been victorious in every instance. The Book of Revelation (12:7–9) prophetically describes one such war in heaven where Michael continues to prevail against Ahriman:

> Now war arose in heaven, Michael and his angels fighting against the dragon; and the dragon and his angels fought, but they were defeated and there was no longer any place for them in heaven. And the great dragon was thrown

down, that ancient serpent, who is called the Devil and Satan, the deceiver of the whole world—he was thrown down to the earth, and his angels were thrown down with him.

Alarmingly, according to the spiritual-scientific research of Rudolf Steiner (and others), this biblically-predicted event recently occurred during the late-nineteenth century. Steiner detailingly described this momentous event in several of his lectures and writings; such as the following example from a lecture given on 27 October 1917 entitled "The Fallen Spirits' Influence in the World":

I have also spoken of the profoundly significant battle which took place in the spiritual regions of the world between the early 1840s and the autumn of 1879. This was one of the battles which occur repeatedly in world and human evolution and are customarily represented by the image of Michael or St. George fighting the dragon. Michael won one such victory over the dragon on behalf of the spiritual worlds in 1879. At that time the spirits of darkness who worked against the Michaelic impulses were cast down from the spiritual realm into the human realms. As I said, from that time onwards they have been active in the feeling, will and mind impulses of human beings. Present-day events can therefore only be understood if one turns the inner eye to the spiritual powers which are now moving among us. (Published in *The Fall of the Spirits of Darkness*, 1993)

As Steiner has indicated, the esoteric fact that malevolent ahrimanic beings have been superphysically cast down to the earth has caused negative repercussions in human thinking, feeling and willing. Even though the nineteenth-century fall of the spirits of darkness significantly opened up the heavenly realm to human entry and experience, their superphysical presence on earth has resulted in increased materialism, atheism, mechanization and radical-socialism (communism). It is imperative that human beings today become increasingly aware of the covert influences of the ahrimanic beings among us. As Steiner has warned:

> On the other hand, the spirits of darkness are now among us. We have to be on guard so that we may realize what is happening when we encounter them and gain a real idea of where they are to be found. The most dangerous thing you can do in the immediate future will be to give yourself up unconsciously to the influences which are definitely present. For it makes no difference to their reality whether they are recognized or unrecognized.
>
> The first step [of the fallen spirits] must be to throw people's views into confusion, turning their concepts and ideas inside out. This is a serious thing and must be watched with care ...
>
> For it was the ideal of the spirits of darkness before 1879, and has been even more so since they walk among us in the human realms since 1879, to spin a web of illusion over human beings and into human brains and let illusions stream through human hearts.
>
> Mephistopheles [aka: Satan, Ahriman], representative of the spirits of darkness, who invents everything humanity has come to depend on and will depend on more and more, especially in the twentieth century.
>
> Spirits of darkness are at work everywhere to befog human minds. One day people will waken from the mists and vapours in which they are now asleep ... (Ibid.)

The pervasive influence of ahrimanic spirits on earth helps to explain and understand the bizarre, modern-day pandemic outbreak of "Trump Derangement Syndrome" and socialist "group-think." In this case, focusing public awareness on earth-bound spirits of darkness is not intended to cause widespread fear and alarm. But rather, it's to awaken somnolent mankind to the imminent supernatural dangers occurring in our midst today; thereby helping concerned individuals prepare and protect themselves.

Furthermore, this life-and-death spiritual battle is raging today whether we like it or not; and whether we are aware of it or not. Moreover, every human being on planet earth and in the heavenly realms is involved in this battle, whether we like it or not; and whether we are aware of it or not. It therefore behooves each and every God-loving person living today to consciously align themselves with Christ-Jesus the saviour, St. Michael the archangel, and all the divine spirits of light in defense of humanity and the entire world.

By remaining ignorant of the spiritual battle taking place, the unwary are more easily manipulated and coerced into evil-complicity by Ahriman and the fallen spirits of darkness.

5.4 The Heavenly Kingdom of Christ-Jesus is Not of This World

Even though Christ-Jesus is the "saviour of the world," and even though after the resurrection "All authority in heaven and on earth has been given to [him]" (Matt 28:18), he has no intention of establishing a socio-political rulership on earth—now or in the future. Our Lord made this abundantly clear when Pilate asked if he was the "king of the Jews"; his unequivocal reply:

> My Kingdom is not an earthly kingdom. If it were, my followers would fight to keep me from being handed over to the Jewish leaders. But my Kingdom is not of this world. (John 18:36)

Moreover, physically ruling over the kingdoms of the earth as a political and military messiah was soundly rejected by Christ-Jesus as one of the three temptations proposed by

Satan in the wilderness. As recorded biblically:

> Again, the devil took him to a very high mountain, and showed him all the kingdoms of the world and the glory of them; and he said to him, "All these I will give you, if you will fall down and worship me." Then Jesus said to him, "Begone, Satan!" (Matt 4:8–10)

In these two biblical instances Christ is obviously emphasizing that his true home—the realm in which his spirit permanently resides—is in the heavenly world. His salvational mission, then, is not to physically establish a utopian society on earth that is under his supernatural control as a political messiah; but to gradually and progressively lead and assist struggling humanity back to a heavenly state of paradise superior to what was lost in the primordial past because of luciferic and ahrimanic interference.

Unlike Lucifer and Ahriman, Christ does not lead through secretive seduction and cunning coercion; but rather, individuals must choose to follow his divine direction entirely through their own free-will. Furthermore, even though Christ's true kingdom is not of this world, this does not mean that he ignores, denigrates or disparages human life on earth. But rather, Christ is also working to gradually transform the earth itself in order to facilitate mankind's heavenly return. This of course will take long ages of evolutionary time to accomplish. As prophetically indicated in Revelation (21:1, 2, 5):

> Then I saw a new heaven and a new earth; for the first heaven and the first earth had passed away, and the sea was no more. And I saw the holy city, new Jerusalem, coming down out of heaven from God ... And [Christ] who sat upon the [heavenly] throne said, "Behold, I make all things new."

Unfortunately, throughout the Christian era there been

those unfortunates who mistakenly believe that Christ at his second coming will materially establish a one-world kingdom on earth, and theocratically rule as a political messiah (some contend for a thousand years). This Christ-rejected falsehood is termed "millenarianism," and has been soundly denounced by the Catholic Church for centuries. As stated in paragraph 676 of the *Catechism of the Catholic Church*:

> The Antichrist's deception already begins to take shape in the world every time the claim is made to realize within history that messianic hope which can only be realized beyond history through the eschatological judgment. The Church has rejected even modified forms of this falsification of the kingdom to come under the name of millenarianism, especially the "intrinsically perverse" political form of a secular messianism.

As clearly implied in the *Catechism* quotation above, any future individual stepping onto the world-stage claiming to be the messiah, and intent on commanding global authority as the political, religious and military ruler of a one-world socialist government will most assuredly be the Antichrist. Alarmingly, the same fundamentalist Christians who are currently sounding the loudest alarm about the dangers of the Antichrist are also millenarianists—that is, they are also unknowingly welcoming and embracing the destined incarnation of the Antichrist—who they believe is the second coming of Christ.

Since Christian fundamentalists mistakenly embrace the erroneous millenarianist vision of a future, worldwide, "Christian" theocratic state, many concerned individuals are understandably worried when President Trump promotes religious freedom or traditional Christian values. Even though a great many fundamentalist Christians support President Trump, thankfully he is not a fundamentalist himself, and is not about to governmentally impose religious ideology—Christian or otherwise—on non-believing citizens who don't welcome it. Obviously, the constitutional right to religious freedom also includes the right not to have religion forcibly imposed on a nation's citizenry. Radical-socialism, on the other hand, has no qualms about legislatively imposing its politically-correct, Marxist group-think ideology on the entire population (as occurred during the socialist Obama years).

Furthermore, as similarly disturbing as that of fundamentalist Christian belief, Jewish believers who have rejected Christ-Jesus as the true messiah; and who are looking instead to a human messianic figure that will rebuild the temple in Jerusalem, claim the throne of King David, reunite the twelve scattered tribes, amass an undefeatable army, conquer all foreign enemies, and establish Israel as the foremost nation on earth—are also unknowingly welcoming the incarnation of the Antichrist.

Vigilant observers can correctly conclude from the foregoing, then, that the Antichrist (Satan) has already deceptively and cunningly amassed a large number of obliviously-deluded supporters and followers prior to his human incarnation.

As the most powerful political figure on the planet, by resisting the forces of globalization; by challenging the pervasive agenda of radical-socialism; by exposing and prosecuting deep-state corruption; by making America economically, culturally and militarily strong again; by defending the innocent lives of unborn children against abortion; and by defending religious freedom and Judeo-Christian civilization—President Donald Trump has knowingly aligned himself, his administration and his dedicated supporters with the Christ-centred forces of divine light.

As such, President Trump is actively, courageously and successfully engaged in the spiritual warfare of the 21st century—particularly against the diabolic forces of Satan

(Ahriman) that are earnestly preparing for his future human incarnation as the Antichrist. All those followers of Christ-Jesus who are also consciously engaged in this spiritual battle continually pray to the Trinitarian God of love for President Trump's divine protection, divine wisdom, divine strength, divine compassion, divine confidence, divine peace and divine success.

CONCLUSION

TO THE SPIRITUALLY-MINDED of today, the world is engulfed in a supernatural battle between the celestial forces of light and the infernal forces of darkness. The ultimate prize?—the fate of mankind and the destiny of planet earth. Arrayed on the side of evil are the legions of Lucifer and Satan; arrayed on the side of divinity are the hosts of Christ-Jesus and St. Michael.

Without a conscious awareness of the supernatural causative agents behind the world of outward events, much of the social upheaval raging throughout the world today is alarming, worrisome and difficult to explain. But with spirit-filled perception, it becomes clear that the radical-socialism insidiously creeping across Western society is more than just a short-term cultural revolution; but an integral part of a long-term clandestine strategy to establish a one-world socialist government.

The strongest opposition to this frightening scenario is Christianity—which explains why today's radical-socialism is rabidly intent on destroying Christianity through increased secular and atheistic ideology; materialistic science and technology; and anti-religious government legislation. Moreover, as the most powerful Christian nation on earth, the United States of America stands directly in the way of this socialist "new world order."

Not surprisingly, then, since the 1960s radical-socialism has been deliberately eroding the strong historical foundations of America in a number of devious ways—through educational indoctrination; through "open-border" Hispanic immigration; through the unvetted influx of Islamic "refugees"; through the off-shoring of American manufacturing; through unfair international trade deals; through government attacks on religious freedom, specifically Christianity; through the steady erosion of sexual morality and the traditional family; through increased federal regulation, taxation and deficit spending; through deep-state government corruption; and through biased mainstream media and social media propaganda.

Even more sinister than the conspiratorial plot to establish a socialist new world order is the spiritual knowledge that this one-world government is not a goal in itself; but rather the long-term preparation for the destined incarnation of the biblical Antichrist—Satan in human form. As the mastermind of this one-world government, the Antichrist intends on controlling mankind and usurping the divine plan for evolution on earth.

The supernatural forces of our saviour Christ-Jesus and St. Michael the archangel are of course battling against the evil intentions of the Antichrist. Numerous Christians and other God-loving persons have willingly enlisted in this spiritual fight. Unfortunately, at this critical time the international power of the Catholic Church has been weakened by the covert installation of a socialist pope—Francis I.

Thankfully, as a crucial counter-balance to this papal corruption, the spiritual forces of the United States have raised up a powerful Christian president instead—Donald J. Trump. By "Making America Great Again," President Trump is actively resisting radical-socialism and the globalizing forces of the new world order. Moreover, as a "warrior of God," President Trump has aligned himself with the Christ-centred forces of the 21st century in their battle against the evil forces of the Antichrist.

APPENDIX

DONALD J. TRUMP, as American president, has delivered some of the most powerfully-inspiring speeches of any president in US history. But because of the seditious, "destroy Trump," mainstream news-media, and the radical-socialist, anti-Trump hysterical mindset, these speeches have not been given the high praise and recognition that they so richly deserve. In time, however, once saner minds have prevailed, these speeches will be extolled as some of the great treasures of American history.

Two examples have been printed here: President Trump's Inaugural Speech delivered on 20 January 2017, and his speech delivered at the National Prayer Breakfast on 2 February 2017. The Inaugural Speech, as a formal address, is included here in full; whereas the Prayer Breakfast speech, being a more informal delivery, has been partially excerpted.

1. President Trump's Inaugural Speech
(20 January 2017)

Chief Justice Roberts, President Carter, President Clinton, President Bush, President Obama, fellow Americans, and people of the world: thank you.

We, the citizens of America, are now joined in a great national effort to rebuild our country and to restore its promise for all of our people.

Together, we will determine the course of America and the world for years to come.

We will face challenges. We will confront hardships. But we will get the job done.

Every four years, we gather on these steps to carry out the orderly and peaceful transfer of power, and we are grateful to President Obama and First Lady Michelle Obama for their gracious aid throughout this transition. They have been magnificent.

Today's ceremony, however, has very special meaning. Because today we are not merely transferring power from one Administration to another, or from one party to another—but we are transferring power from Washington, D.C. and giving it back to you, the American People.

For too long, a small group in our nation's Capital has reaped the rewards of government while the people have borne the cost.

Washington flourished—but the people did not share in its wealth.

Politicians prospered—but the jobs left, and the factories closed.

The establishment protected itself, but not the citizens of our country.

Their victories have not been your victories; their triumphs have not been your triumphs; and while they celebrated in our nation's Capital, there was little to celebrate for struggling families all across our land.

That all changes—starting right here, and right now, because this moment is your moment: it belongs to you.

It belongs to everyone gathered here today and everyone watching all across America.

This is your day. This is your celebration.

And this, the United States of America, is your country.

What truly matters is not which party controls our government, but whether our government is controlled by the people.

January 20th 2017, will be remembered as the day the people became the rulers of this nation again.

The forgotten men and women of our country will be forgotten no longer.

Everyone is listening to you now.

You came by the tens of millions to become part of a historic movement the likes of which the world has never seen before.

At the center of this movement is a crucial conviction: that a nation exists to serve its citizens.

Americans want great schools for their children, safe neighborhoods for their families, and good jobs for themselves.

These are the just and reasonable demands of a righteous public.

But for too many of our citizens, a different reality exists: Mothers and children trapped in poverty in our inner cities; rusted-out factories scattered like tombstones across the landscape of our nation; an education system, flush with cash, but which leaves our young and beautiful students deprived of knowledge; and the crime and gangs and drugs that have stolen too many lives and robbed our country of so much unrealized potential.

This American carnage stops right here and stops right now.

We are one nation—and their pain is our pain. Their dreams are our dreams; and their success will be our success. We share one heart, one home, and one glorious destiny.

The oath of office I take today is an oath of allegiance to all Americans.

For many decades, we've enriched foreign industry at the expense of American industry;

Subsidized the armies of other countries while allowing for the very sad depletion of our military;

We've defended other nation's borders while refusing to defend our own;

And spent trillions of dollars overseas while America's infrastructure has fallen into disrepair and decay.

We've made other countries rich while the wealth, strength, and confidence of our country has disappeared over the horizon.

One by one, the factories shuttered and left our shores, with not even a thought about the millions upon millions of American workers left behind.

The wealth of our middle class has been ripped from their homes and then redistributed across the entire world.

But that is the past. And now we are looking only to the future.

We assembled here today are issuing a new decree to be heard in every city, in every foreign capital, and in every hall of power.

From this day forward, a new vision will govern our land.

From this moment on, it's going to be America First.

Every decision on trade, on taxes, on immigration, on foreign affairs, will be made to benefit American workers and American families.

We must protect our borders from the ravages of other countries making our products, stealing our companies, and destroying our jobs. Protection will lead to great prosperity and strength.

I will fight for you with every breath in my body—and I will never, ever let you down.

America will start winning again, winning like never before.

We will bring back our jobs. We will bring back our

borders. We will bring back our wealth. And we will bring back our dreams.

We will build new roads, and highways, and bridges, and airports, and tunnels, and railways all across our wonderful nation.

We will get our people off of welfare and back to work—rebuilding our country with American hands and American labor.

We will follow two simple rules: Buy American and Hire American.

We will seek friendship and goodwill with the nations of the world—but we do so with the understanding that it is the right of all nations to put their own interests first.

We do not seek to impose our way of life on anyone, but rather to let it shine as an example for everyone to follow.

We will reinforce old alliances and form new ones—and unite the civilized world against Radical Islamic Terrorism, which we will eradicate completely from the face of the Earth.

At the bedrock of our politics will be a total allegiance to the United States of America, and through our loyalty to our country, we will rediscover our loyalty to each other.

When you open your heart to patriotism, there is no room for prejudice.

The Bible tells us, "how good and pleasant it is when God's people live together in unity."

We must speak our minds openly, debate our disagreements honestly, but always pursue solidarity.

When America is united, America is totally unstoppable.

There should be no fear—we are protected, and we will always be protected.

We will be protected by the great men and women of our military and law enforcement and, most importantly, we are protected by God.

Finally, we must think big and dream even bigger.

In America, we understand that a nation is only living as long as it is striving.

We will no longer accept politicians who are all talk and no action—constantly complaining but never doing anything about it.

The time for empty talk is over.

Now arrives the hour of action.

Do not let anyone tell you it cannot be done. No challenge can match the heart and fight and spirit of America.

We will not fail. Our country will thrive and prosper again.

We stand at the birth of a new millennium, ready to unlock the mysteries of space, to free the Earth from the miseries of disease, and to harness the energies, industries and technologies of tomorrow.

A new national pride will stir our souls, lift our sights, and heal our divisions.

It is time to remember that old wisdom our soldiers will never forget: that whether we are black or brown or white, we all bleed the same red blood of patriots, we all enjoy the same glorious freedoms, and we all salute the same great American Flag.

And whether a child is born in the urban sprawl of Detroit or the windswept plains of Nebraska, they look up at the same night sky, they fill their heart with the same dreams, and they are infused with the breath of life by the same almighty Creator.

So to all Americans, in every city near and far, small and large, from mountain to mountain, and from ocean to ocean, hear these words:

You will never be ignored again.

Your voice, your hopes, and your dreams, will define our American destiny. And your courage and goodness and love will forever guide us along the way.

Together, We Will Make America Strong Again.

We Will Make America Wealthy Again.

We Will Make America Proud Again.
We Will Make America Safe Again.
And, Yes, Together, We Will Make America Great Again.
Thank you, God Bless You, And God Bless America.

2. President Trump's Speech at the National Prayer Breakfast (2 February 2017)

But most importantly, I want to thank the American people. Your faith and prayers have sustained me and inspired me through some very, very tough times. All around America I have met amazing people whose words of worship and encouragement has a constant source of strength. What I hear most often as I travel the country are five words that never, ever fail to touch my heart. That's "I am praying for you." I hear it so often. "I am praying for you, Mr. President." No one has inspired me more in my travels than the families of the United States military. Men and women who put their lives on the line every day for their country and their countrymen.

I just came back yesterday from Dover Air Force Base to join the family of Chief William Ryan Owens as America's fallen hero was returned home. Very, very sad, but very, very beautiful. Very, very beautiful. His family was there. Incredible family. Loved him so much. So devastated. He was so devastated. But the ceremony was amazing. He died in defense of our nation. He gave his life in defense of our people. Our debt to him and our debt to his family is eternal and everlasting. Greater love hath no man than this that a man lay down his life for his friends. We will never forget the men and women who wear the uniform. Believe me.

From generation to generation, their vigilance has kept our liberty alive. Our freedom is won by their sacrifice and our security has been earned with their sweat and blood and tears.

God has blessed this land to give us such incredible heroes and patriots. They are very, very special, and we are going to take care of them. Our soldiers understand that what matters is not party or ideology or creed, but the bonds of loyalty that link us all together as one. America is a nation of believers. In towns all across our land it is plain to see what we easily forget—so easily we forget this—that the quality of our lives is not defined by our material success, but our spiritual success. I will tell you that. And I tell you that from somebody that has had material success and knows tremendous numbers of people with great material success—the most material success. Many of those people are very, very miserable, unhappy people. And I know a lot of people without that, but they have great families. They have great faith. They don't have money—at least not nearly to the extent—and they are happy. Those, to me, are the successful people, I have to tell you.

I was blessed to be raised in a churched home. My mother and father taught me that to whom much is given, much is expected. I was sworn in on the very bible from which my mother would teach as young children. And that faith lives on in my heart every single day. The people in this room come from many, many backgrounds. You represent so many religions and so many views. But we are all united by our faith in our creator and our firm knowledge that we are all equal in His eyes. We are not just flesh and bone and blood. We are human beings with souls. Our republic was formed on the basis that freedom is not a gift from government, but that freedom is a gift from God.

It was the great Thomas Jefferson who said the God who gave us life gave us liberty. Jefferson asked, "Can the liberties of a nation be secure when we have removed a conviction that these liberties are the gift of God?" Among those freedoms is the right to worship according to our own beliefs. That is why I will get rid and totally destroy the Johnson Amendment and allow our representatives of faith to speak freely and without fear of retribution. I will do that. Remember.

Freedom of religion is a sacred right, but also a right under threat all around us and the world is under serious, serious threat in so many different ways. And I've never seen it so much and so openly since I took the position of president. The world is in trouble, but we are going to straighten it out. OK? That's what I do. I fix things. We are going to straighten it out. Believe me. When you hear about the tough telephone calls I'm having, don't worry about it. Just don't worry about it. They're tough. We have to be tough. It's time we're going to be a little tough, folks.

We're taken advantage of by every nation in the world, virtually. It's not going to happen anymore. It's not going to happen anymore. We have seen unimaginable violence carried out in the name of religion. Acts of wanton slaughter against religious minorities, horrors on a scale that defy description. Terrorism is a fundamental threat to religious freedom. It must be stopped, and it will be stopped. It may not be pretty for a little while. It will be stopped ... You watch. You just watch. Things will be different. We have seen peace-loving Muslims brutalized, victimized, murdered and oppressed by ISIS killers. We have seen threats of extermination against the Jewish people. We have seen a campaign of ISIS and genocide against Christians where they cut off heads. Not since the Middle Ages have we seen that. We haven't seen that. The cutting off of heads. Now they cut off the heads. They drown people in steel cages. I haven't seen this—nobody's seen this—for many, many years.

All nations have a moral obligation to speak out against such violence. All nations have a duty to work together to confront it, viciously, if we have to. So I want to express clearly today to the American people that my administration will do everything in its power to defend and protect religious liberty in our land. America must forever remain a tolerant society where all faiths are respected and where all of our citizens can feel safe and secure. We have to feel safe and secure. In recent days, we have begun to take necessary action to achieve the goal. Our nation has the most generous immigration system in the world. But these are those and there are those that would exploit that generosity to undermine the values that we hold so dear. We need security. There are those who would seek to enter the country for the purpose of spreading violence or oppressing other people based upon their faith or their lifestyle. Not right.

We will not allow a beachhead of intolerance to spread in our nation. You look all over the world and you see what's happening. So in the coming days, we will develop a system to help ensure that those admitted into our country fully embrace our values of religious and personal liberty. And that they reject any form of oppression and discrimination. We want people to come into our nation. But we want people to love us and to love our values. Not to hate us and to hate our values. We will be a safe country. We will be a free country and we will be a country where all citizens can practice their beliefs without fear of hostility or fear of violence.

America will flourish as long as our liberty and in particular our religious liberty is allowed to flourish. America will succeed as long as our most vulnerable citizens—and we have some that are so vulnerable—have a path to success. And America will thrive as long as we continue to have faith in each other and faith in God. That faith in God has inspired men and women to sacrifice for the needy, to deploy to wars overseas and to lock arms at home to ensure equal rights for every man, woman and child in our land. It is that faith that sent the pilgrims across oceans, the pioneers across the plains and the young people all across America to chase their dreams. They are chasing their dreams. We are going to bring those dreams back.

As long as we have God, we are never, ever alone.

Whether it is soldier on the night watch or the single parent on the night shift, God will always give us solace and strength and comfort. We need to carry on and to keep carrying on. For us here in Washington, we must never, ever stop asking God for the wisdom to serve the public according to His will. That is why President Eisenhower and Sen. Carlson had the wisdom to gather together 64 years ago to begin this truly great tradition. But that is not all they did together. Let me tell you the rest of the story. Just one year later, Sen. Carlson was among the members of Congress to send to the president's desk a joint resolution that added "Under God" to our Pledge of Allegiance. It's a great thing. Because that is what we are and that is what we will always be and that is what our people want—one beautiful nation under God. Thank you. God bless you. And God bless America. Thank you.

NOTES

INTRODUCTION

1. The Eastern Bloc States are European nations that the Soviet Union, under Joseph Stalin, invaded and annexed during and after the Second World War. For more information, please refer to Chapter 3, sub-chapter 3.4.
2. This is a reference to the communist ideology that was developed by Karl Marx (1818–1883) and Friedrich Engels (1820–1895) in such works as *The Communist Manifesto* (1848). More information on Marxism is available throughout Chapter 1.
3. For more specific information on George Soros, please refer to Chapter 3, sub-chapter 3.6; as well as the associated chapter notes.
4. The New World Order is discussed in greater detail in Chapter 3, sub-chapter 3.8.

CHAPTER 1

5. Simply defined, laissez-faire capitalism is an economic

system in which private business transactions are free from government interference and intervention, such as regulations, subsidies, tax concessions and tariffs.

6. The New Democratic Party in Canada developed out of the Co-operative Commonwealth Federation (CCF), a democratic-socialist political party founded in 1932. As with the nineteenth-century socialist movement in England, many influential leaders of the CCF were devout Christians. The Federation's first leader, J. S. Woodsworth (1874–1942), for example, was a Methodist minister before becoming politically active.

A much more famous CCF member was Tommy Douglas (1904–1986) who was a Baptist minister before becoming the premier of Saskatchewan from 1944 to 1961. Douglas' government was the first democratic-socialist government in North America. He is best known in Canada for introducing the continent's first universal health care program.

7. "Transgender activists" refers to sex-activists who subscribe to "gender theory," the irrational notion that male and female sexual distinctions are nothing more than social constructs; and which can be interchangeably transmorphed through radical surgery and hormone treatment.

CHAPTER 2

8. As a disturbing indication as to how far sexual morality has declined in Western society since the start of the sexual revolution, bestiality (or "zoophilia") is no longer illegal in many states in America, such as Nevada, New Hampshire, New Mexico, Ohio, Texas, Vermont, West Virginia and Wyoming. Even more appalling, "bestiality brothels" or "erotic zoos" are popular in Germany,

Denmark and Hungary as a "lifestyle choice."

Moreover, as recently as 2016, the Supreme Court of Canada in a controversial bestiality ruling declared that most sex acts between people and animals are legal, as long as no penetration is involved. Appallingly, the main objection to this unsettling ruling was not on the grounds of sexual perversion; but by animal rights groups on the grounds that animals were being exploited for sexual gratification.

9. A Vox poll conducted in 2015 found that only 18% of Americans self-identified as being feminist; a sharp decline from the 33% in 1992. Even lower in Britain, a 2015 survey by the Fawcett Society found that only 7% of those questioned self-identified as being feminist.

10. "KKKist" refers to the Ku Klux Klan, an extreme White supremacy group founded in the southern United States during the mid-1800s.

11. Canadian economist and humorist Stephen Leacock (1869–1944) concluded that socialism (communism) was doomed to failure because human beings lacked the necessary level of moral goodness. He consequently wrote: "But this socialism, this communism, would only work in Heaven where they don't need it, or in Hell where they have it already."

CHAPTER 3

12. George Soros was originally born in 1930 as György Schwartz to an affluent Jewish family in Budapest, Hungary. He survived the Holocaust of World War II by secretly posing as the godson of a non-Jewish government official who was a Nazi collaborator. As a teenager, young George unapologetically and unremorsefully assisted his government "godfather" with

NOTES

the Nazi confiscation of Jewish property.

In 1947 Soros inexplicably immigrated to England and somehow managed to enroll in the London School of Economics; earning a Bachelor of Science in philosophy in 1951, and a Master of Science in philosophy in 1954. After graduation he began his financial career at a merchant bank in London, then moved to New York in 1954. As a Wall Street trader specializing in European stocks, Soros slowly worked his way up to starting his own offshore hedge fund in 1969.

By using other people's money to invest and by exhibiting a ruthless and amoral talent for currency manipulation, Soros in 2016 had acquired a staggering net worth of about $25 billion. Along the way he crashed the British pound in 1992 by dumping 10 billion sterling; thereby acquiring his first ill-gotten billion-dollar profit. Later in 1997 during the Asian financial crisis, Soros was called an "unscrupulous profiteer" by Malaysian Prime Minister Mahathir bin Mohamad for abasing the nation's currency through his devious trading tactics. In Thailand Soros was also described as "an economic war criminal."

In 1998, Soros was implicated in the orchestrated collapse of the Russian economy; and used the devalued ruble and his insider access as an opportunity to buy up some cheap Russian oil. Previously, in a 1994 interview for the *New Republic*, Soros egotistically implied that it was his political and economic machinations that caused the collapse of the Soviet Union—and that "the former Soviet Empire is now called the Soros Empire."

In 2002 Soros was convicted of felony insider trading in France, and was ordered to pay $2.9 billion in restitution. In 2009, Hungary fined Soros $2.2 million for "illegal market manipulation." Moreover, Hungary's top education official, Minister of Human Capacities Zoltan Balog has stated: "We are committed to use all legal means at our disposal to stop pseudo-civil society spy groups such as the ones funded by George Soros." As recently as 2017, a $10 billion lawsuit accuses Soros of meddling in the governmental politics of Guinea in order to "freeze Israeli company BSG Resources out of the West African nation's lucrative iron ore mining contracts."

13. In 2003, Soros decided that removing George W. Bush as US President had become the "central focus" of his life, which he described as "a matter of life and death." To help ensure that Democratic Senator John Kerry would become the next president in 2004, Soros contributing almost $24 million to advocacy groups that supported Kerry (according to the Center for Responsive Politics).

When Kerry lost, a discouraged Soros turned his attention to electing Barak Obama in 2008. According to a 2012 article in *The New Yorker*, Soros gave $5 million to help elect Obama (though he later regrets that he didn't back Hillary Clinton instead).

14. To describe George Soros as "egomaniacal" is in no way an extreme exaggeration. On several occasions Soros has unabashedly stated that he considers himself as "some kind of god." In his book *The Alchemy of Finance* (1987), for example, Soros wrote:

> I admit that I have always harbored an exaggerated view of self-importance—to put it bluntly, I fancied myself as some kind of god.

Later in 1993, Soros told the British newspaper *The Independent*:

> It is a sort of disease when you consider yourself some kind of god, the creator of everything, but I feel comfortable about it now since I began to live it out.

Soros also indicated to his biographer, Michael Kaufman, that he regards himself as the "the conscience of the world." Who but a deluded megalomaniac would think that he alone was responsible for determining what is right and wrong, good and bad for the entire world?

15. In US politics, "dark money" is anonymous, unlimited and undisclosed money donated to non-profit groups that is often used to secretly affect politicians, elections, public-opinion and social policy.

16. Soros' geopolitical interference even extends to the United Nations and to the Vatican.

17. GDP or gross domestic product is a monetary measure of the market value of all goods and services produced by a country during a particular period of time (usually yearly or quarterly). GDP measures are useful in determining and comparing economic performance between counties.

18. Because of political interference in the 2014 Ukrainian uprising, two of Soros' non-profit groups were deemed "undesirable" by the Russian state, and ignominiously kicked out of the country. In a statement released at the time:

> It was found that the activity of the Open Society Foundations and the Open Society Institute Assistance Foundation represents a threat to the foundations of the constitutional system of the Russian Federation and the security of the state.

Even if it could be argued that these Soros-funded non-profits were on Ukrainian soil honestly promoting Western democracy; the point is, that is the job of government agencies such as the US State Department—not private foreign billionaires like George Soros.

19. The radical-left like to pretentiously think of themselves as "progressive"; and that their socialist agenda is

profoundly furthering human progress. In reality, their intolerant, politically-correct, group-think world-view is destructive to positive social development and better described as "regressive."

20. Some of the profusion of leftist organizations that Soros funds through his Open Society Foundations are: Black Lives Matter, Planned Parenthood, the Clinton Foundation, Media Matters, MoveOn.org, Center for American Progress, Climate Policy Initiative, and America Coming.

21. Though the Bank of Canada was originally established in 1934 as a privately-owned corporation, it was later re-designated in 1938 as a federal Crown corporation legislatively owned by the Minister of Finance on behalf of the Canadian government. The bank is independently managed by a government-appointed board of directors under the leadership of a governor.

22. Adam Smith (1723–1790), the "father of modern economics," in *The Wealth of Nations* (1776) expressed a similar sentiment regarding businessmen in general:

> People of the same trade seldom meet together, even for merriment and diversion, but the conversation ends in a conspiracy against the public, or in some contrivance to raise prices.

23. The covert use of the Bank for International Settlements by Nazi Germany during World War II should come as no surprise considering that a number of prominent Nazi officials sat on the BIS board of directors between 1933 and 1945—such as: Walther Funk (the Reich Minister of Economic Affairs), Emil Puhl (a Nazi economist and bank official), Hermann Schmitz (a German industrialist and Nazi war criminal), and Kurt Baron von Schroeder (German financier and Nazi war criminal).

24. The 60 central-bank members of the BIS demonstrate a

broad representation from around the world: 35 are from Europe, 13 are from Asia, 5 are from South America, 3 are from North America, 2 are from Oceania, and 2 are from Africa.

25. Since 2008, Goldman Sachs switched from being an "investment bank" to being a "bank holding company." While there exists a Goldman Sachs Bank USA (GS Bank), it is a subsidiary of Goldman Sachs Group, Inc; which is still described as a world leader in investment banking and securities, with specialization in global investment banking.

26. "Maoist" refers to Mao Zedong (1893–1976), the infamous Chinese communist who established the dictatorial People's Republic of China. "Trotskyist" refers to Leon Trotsky (1879–1940), a leading Russian revolutionary who developed his own version of Marxist communism called "Trotskyism."

27. "Patristic writings" is a reference to the writings of the early Apostolic or Church Fathers; such as St. Augustine of Hippo, St. Jerome, St. Ignatius of Antioch and St. Athanasius of Alexandria.

28. In a 2017 interview in the leftist Spanish daily *El Pais*, Pope Francis openly declared that:

> Liberation theology was a good thing for Latin America ... Liberation theology had positive aspects and also had deviations, especially on the part of the Marxist analysis of reality.

29. In 1985, John Paul II also denounced Catholic priest Ernesto Cardenal for his involvement in the communist Sandinista government as minister of culture; and his Jesuit brother Fernando Cardenal (1934–2016) for his involvement as minister of education.

30. There is some reasonable evidence that the unusual "retirement" of Benedict XVI, and the speedy installation

of Jorge Bergoglio as Francis I was in the manner of a Vatican "palace coup."

From 1996 to 2006, a group of left-wing bishops, archbishops and cardinals—known as the St. Gallen Group—had been secretly meeting in Switzerland with the sole purpose of radically transforming the Church in an effort to make it "much more modern" [that is, "leftist"]. Their intention, then, was to   prevent the staunchly conservative Cardinal Ratzinger from succeeding John Paul II; and instead, replace him with the socialist archbishop, Jorge Bergoglio.

Unfortunately for the St. Gallen Group, Ratzinger was elected as Pope Benedict XVI in 2005, with Bergoglio coming in second. But as it "happened," Benedict mysteriously resigned eight years later, to be replaced by Bergoglio as Francis I.

Some of the high-profile members of this subversive Church group were Belgian cardinal Godfried Danneels, Italian cardinals Carlo Maria Martini and Achille Silvestrini, Dutch bishop Adriaan Van Luyn, German cardinals Walter Kasper and Karl Lehman, and Britain's cardinal Basil Hume.

31. In January 2017, a small group of well-respected Catholic lay leaders sent a letter of concern to President Trump (and published in *The Remnant*) regarding the questionable installation and socialist behaviour of Pope Francis. In the letter they state:

> [W]e find that Pope Benedict XVI abdicated under highly unusual circumstances and was replaced by a pope whose apparent mission is to provide a spiritual component to the radical ideological agenda of the international left.

> We remain puzzled by the behavior of this ideologically charged Pope, whose mission seems to

be one of advancing secular agendas of the left rather than guiding the Catholic Church in Her sacred mission … It is simply not the proper role of a Pope to be involved in politics to the point that he is considered to be the leader of the international left.

32. While it is not unusual for rabid critics of the Catholic Church to denounce every pope as an "anti-pope" or "false pope"—or even the "Antichrist"—it is unusual for devoted, practicing Catholics to question, "Is the Pope Catholic?" Unfortunately, the serious concern among American Catholics regarding Francis' heterodoxy has become so widespread that, in 2016, Jesuit-run Fordham University actually did host a panel of Catholic experts to discuss the once unheard of question—"Is the Pope Catholic?"

Moreover, a 2018 Pew Research Center study indicated a growing discontent with Pope Francis. American Catholics who consider the pope "too liberal" has almost doubled from 19% in 2015 to 34% in 2018. Additionally, those who consider him to be "naïve" rose sharply from 15% to 24% during the same period.

33. In a 2013 audience with the pope that was attended by 5000 journalists, Francis declared: "How I would like a church that is poor and for the poor."

34. In 1976, prior to becoming pope, Cardinal Karol Wojtyla prophetically warned about the near-future rise of an "anti-Church" that would preach an "anti-Gospel":

> We are now standing in the face of the greatest historical confrontation humanity has gone through. I do not think that wide circles of the American society or wide circles of the Christian community realize this fully. We are now facing the final confrontation between the Church and the anti-Church, of the Gospel versus the anti-Gospel.

Venerable Fulton J. Sheen (1895–1975) also prophetically described a socialist-style false Church of the future that would be created by an apostate bishop:

> The false Church will be worldly, ecumenical, and global. It will be a loose federation of churches. And religions forming some type of global association. A world parliament of churches.

Blessed Anne Catherine Emmerich (1774–1824) also made some detailed prophecies concerning the future rise of a false Church:

> It was as if people were splitting into two camps ... I saw also the relationship between the two popes ... I saw how baleful would be the consequences of this false Church ... I saw that the Church of Peter was undermined by a plan evolved by the secret sect ... They built a large, singular, extravagant Church which was to embrace all creeds with equal rights: evangelicals, Catholics, and all denominations; a true communion of the unholy with one shepherd and one flock ... I saw the fatal consequences of this counterfeit Church: I saw it increase; I saw heretics of all kinds...

35. Another ultra-connected, left-wing globalist insider worth noting here is Peter Sutherland (1946–2018). Sutherland began his political career as attorney general of Ireland, then moved on to become European Commissioner for Competition, director-general of the World Trade Organization, chairman of Goldman Sachs International, and chairman of British Petroleum.

    As the UN special representative for International Migration, Sutherland strongly promoted unrestricted immigration into the European Union and the U.S. As one commentator has observed, even though most of

Sutherland's positions were "not elected, he has had far greater political impact in the past two decades than almost all of the democratically elected leaders." Sutherland has also been described as "the father of globalization." He was also a member of some other more secretive globalist organizations, such as the Bilderberg Group and the Trilateral Commission.

In 2014, Sutherland acted as financial advisor to the Vatican in an effort to assist Pope Francis in reforming the Vatican's banking and financial systems after a series of scandals.

36. Elizabeth Yore has characterized the United Nations Millennium Development Goals as "controversial, abortion laden, gender bending, feminist driven"—hardly the kind of goals that Pope Francis should be supporting.

37. As an engineer, Gustave Eiffel is perhaps better known for designing and constructing the world-famous Eiffel Tower, which was erected for the 1889 Universal Exposition in Paris.

38. As further indicated by Freemason Todd E. Creason on a website called "The Midnight Freemasons:

> However, there is some evidence that indicates [Thomas Jefferson] may have been a Mason and that he attended Masonic meetings. Dr. Joseph Guillotin reported that he attended meetings at the prestigious Lodge of Nine Muses in Paris, France—the same lodge attended by Voltaire, Benjamin Franklin, and John Paul Jones. He marched in a Masonic procession with Widow's Son Lodge No. 60 and Charlottesville Lodge No. 90 on October 6, 1817, and participated in laying the cornerstone for Central College (now known as the University of Virginia). In 1801, twenty-five years prior to his death, a lodge was chartered in Surry Court House, Virginia—it was named Jefferson Lodge No. 65. And most notably,

upon his death on July 4, 1826, both the Grand Lodge of South Carolina and the Grand Lodge of Louisiana held Masonic funeral rites and processions for him.

39. It is still historically unclear as to why the Great Pyramid of Khufu in Egypt is without a capstone (or pyramidion). Was it always missing; or was it destroyed or stolen? Was it removed by an Arab sultan in AD 1356, along with the outer encasement of highly-polished, smooth white limestone in order to build mosques and fortresses in nearby Cairo? According to one legend, the missing capstone was a smaller, perfectly-proportioned pyramid of black stone, probably onyx.

40. This quotation is from the United States Declaration of Independence.

41. This quotation is from the Constitution of the United States.

42. The official story of the Great Seal motto, "Novus Ordo Seclorum" is that it was coined in 1782 by Charles Thomson (1729–1824). He supposedly adapted it from the following line in a pastoral poem by Virgil (70 BC–19 BC), entitled *Eclogue IV*: "Magnus ab integro seclorum nascitur ordo."

For some puzzling, unexplained reason, the commonly-preferred translation of "Novus Ordo Seclorum" is "New Order of the Ages." This interpretation isn't necessarily incorrect; but it makes no sense whatsoever. The differences in translation have to do with the Latin word, "seclorum." The noun seclorum is the genitive plural of "seclum," which is a rare, poetic form of "seculum" or "saeculum." The problem with seculum is that it has a multiplicity of meanings: race, breed, generation, lifetime, time, century, worldliness—as well as age and world.

As to which particular word to use, a "New-World

[Social] Order" makes much better sense in describing the newly-established Republic of the United States in North America, than does the amorphous "New-[Social] Order for the Ages"—what "Ages"? One cynical reason for the use of "ages" is of course to fend off the hordes of irrational conspiracy theorists and their delusion musings concerning a New World Order.

Interestingly, the English word "secular" is etymologically derived from seculum, and has very similar multiple meanings; such as: temporal, non-religious, non-clerical, non-monastic, occurring once or continuously in a century, relating to a long term of indefinite duration—as well as worldly (of the world), and occurring once or continuously in an age.

43. As evocatively described on 27 November 1915 by American philosopher, diplomat, and educator Nicholas Murray Butler (1862–1947) in an address delivered before the Union League of Philadelphia:

> The old world order changed when this war-storm broke. The old international order passed away as suddenly, as unexpectedly, and as completely as if it had been wiped out by a gigantic flood, by a great tempest, or by a volcanic eruption. The old world order died with the setting of that day's sun and a new world order is being born while I speak, with birth-pangs so terrible that it seems almost incredible that life could come out of such fearful suffering and such overwhelming sorrow.

44. Previous to Bush's 1991 speech, US National Security Advisor Brent Scowcroft stated in 1990: "We believe we are creating the beginning of a new world order coming out of the collapse of the US-Soviet antagonisms." (quoted in the *Washington Post*; May 1991).

45. Although the phrase, "new world order" was used in the

post-World War II years prior to the end of the Cold War, it's not exactly certain what was meant, other than perhaps the "liberal world order." In 1967, for instance, US Senator Robert Kennedy (1925–1968) stated: "All of us will ultimately be judged on the effort we have contributed to building a new world order." Also in 1967, prior to his presidency, Richard Nixon (1913–1994) is quoted in *Foreign Affairs* as saying:

> The developing coherence of Asian regional thinking is reflected in a disposition to consider problems and loyalties in regional terms, and to evolve regional approaches to development needs and to the evolution of a new world order.

Even Pope Paul VI in 1967 wrote in the papal encyclical, *Populorum Progressio*:

> Who can fail to see the need and importance of thus gradually coming to the establishment of a world authority capable of taking effective action on the juridical and political planes? Delegates to international organizations, public officials, gentlemen of the press, teachers and educators—all of you must realize that you have your part to play in the construction of a new world order.

46. Some famous supporters of the World Federalist Movement include Albert Einstein, Winston Churchill, Mahatma Gandhi, Albert Camus, Martin Luther King Jr., Wendell Willkie, Jawaharlal Nehru, Bertrand Russell, Peter Ustinov and Walter Cronkite.

CHAPTER 4

47. The profound and lasting contribution of St. Paul to

today's Christianity was well expressed by James D. Tabor in a *Huffington Post* article entitled "Christianity Before Paul" (2012):

> Visit any church service, Roman Catholic, Protestant or Greek Orthodox, and it is the apostle Paul and his ideas that are central—in the hymns, the creeds, the sermons, the invocation and benediction, and of course, the rituals of baptism and the Holy Communion or Mass. Whether birth, baptism, confirmation, marriage or death, it is predominantly Paul who is evoked to express meaning and significance.

48. A similarly-outlandish Trump prophecy was made in 2011 by retired Florida firefighter Mark Taylor. Taylor made his prophecy public in 18 April 2016 on TruNews (a Christian broadcasting ministry founded and anchored by Rick Wiles). The prophecy stated in part:

> The Spirit of God says I've chosen this man Donald Trump for such a time as this. For as Benjamin Netanyahu is to Israel, so shall this man be to the United States of America, for I will use this man to bring honor, respect and restoration to America. America will be respected once again as the most powerful, prosperous nation on Earth other than Israel. The dollar will be the strongest it has ever been in the history of the United States and will once again be the currency by which all others are judged ... They will say things about this man, the enemy, but it will not affect him and they will say it rolls off of him like a duck. For even as the feathers of a duck protect it, so shall my feathers protect this next president.

Taylor has also co-authored a book entitled *The Trump Prophecies* (2017), and a movie entitled "The Trump

Prophecy" is scheduled for release in October 2018.

49. Rabid, anti-union multi-billionaires, Charles and David Koch, have long been covert bankrollers of Republican politicians and libertarian think-tanks. They have disdainfully regarded politicians as merely "actors playing out a script"; and of course it's been the Koch brothers' intention to "supply the themes and words for the scripts."

One recent example of a Koch political payout occurred in November 2017. After the US House of Representatives passed the sweeping GOP tax reform bill, Charles Koch (and his wife Elizabeth) rewarded Republican House Speaker Paul Ryan with a combined mega-donation of $500,000 towards his fundraising campaign (even though Ryan isn't running for office in November 2018).

As a colourfully-symbolic gesture that he rejects any compromising money from the Koch brothers, on New Year's Eve 2016, President-elect Donald Trump kicked David Koch (and sleazy biographer, Harry Hurt) off his West Palm Beach golf course. Moreover, in various tweets, President Trump has repeatedly stated that he spurns any financial influencing from the Koch brothers; as stated in the following:

> I really like the Koch Brothers (members of my P.B. Club), but I don't want their money or anything else from them. Cannot influence Trump! (2015)

> I turned down a meeting with Charles and David Koch. Much better for them to meet with the puppets of politics [such as Marco Rubio], they will do much better! (2016)

50. Other "Destroy-Trump," fake-news media outlets that the public needs to be aware of are: Rolling Stone, BBC News, Financial Times, Politico, New York Daily News,

L.A. Times, USA Today, US News & World Report, CBC, Newsweek, Time, Yahoo News, PBS, New Yorker, Buzzfeed, MoveOn, Center for American Progress and The Economist.

51. One such failed assassination attempt occurred in 2016—even before Trump was elected president—at a campaign rally in Las Vegas. A deranged twenty-year-old British citizen named Michael Sandford, who was in the US illegally, attempted to grab a local police officer's holstered gun in order to shoot Donald Trump at the event.

Moreover, in January 2016, an unstable Florida man named Dominic Puopolo Jr. was arrested for plotting to assassinate President-elect Trump during the inauguration ceremony. Interestingly, Puopolo Jr. and his family are friends with Bill and Hillary Clinton; and he is known to have previously donated $20,000 to the Democratic National Committee.

52. The contemptuous, supercilious and condescending attitude of the establishment elites towards middle-Americans was best exemplified by failed Democratic presidential candidate Hillary Clinton at a 2016 campaign fundraising event, when she referred to Trump supporters as a "basket of deplorables."

53. In *The Art of the Deal* (1987), Trump has similarly stated:

> The worst thing you can possibly do in a deal is seem desperate to make it. That makes the other guy smell blood, and then you're dead. The best thing you can do is deal from strength, and leverage is the biggest strength you can have. Leverage is having something the other guy wants. Or better yet, needs. Or best of all, simply can't do without.

54. As Trump has expressed in his book quoted above:

> You can't con people, at least not for long. You can

create excitement, you can do wonderful promotion and get all kinds of press, and you can throw in a little hyperbole. But if you can't deliver the goods, people will eventually catch on.

55. Immediately following a 2018 G7 Summit meeting, Canadian Prime Minister Justin Trudeau demonstrated his diplomatic inexperience and juvenile leadership by blustering as a Canadian tough-guy and publicly announcing retaliatory tariffs against the US, after being openly "friendly" with President Trump during the Summit.

   Not surprisingly, this unexpected maneuver negated any goodwill that was gained at the Summit, and was regarded as a "backstabbing" attack on President Trump, who later described Trudeau as "very dishonest and weak." As a result, Trump withdrew US support of a jointly agreed-on G7 communiqué. President Trump had already removed any obfuscating language concerning abortion in the feminist-promoting document.

   In the scathing words of presidential trade advisor Peter Navarro:

   > There's a special place in hell for any foreign leader that engages in bad faith diplomacy with President Donald J. Trump and then tries to stab him in the back on the way out the door, and that's what bad faith Justin Trudeau did with that stunt press conference.

56. While holdover Obama loyalists incredulously attempt to take credit for Trump's victory over ISIS, even crooked CIA Director John Brennan admitted in a 2015 speech that the Islamic State terror group increased by about 4,400 percent during Barack Obama's presidency.

57. More specifically, Fox News currently has almost twice the prime time viewers that MSNBC has; and almost

three times that of CNN. Even among the 25–54 age group that is most targeted by advertisers, Fox News has a commanding lead. Of the top five cable news shows, Fox News has four out of the five; with Sean Hannity being the highest-rated host, having almost a million more viewers than MSNBC's Rachel Maddow.

58. If Steele was actually sourcing "high-level Kremlin officials," it is extremely unlikely that these officials would willingly share sensitive intel-info with a British ex-spy without Vladimir Putin knowing about it. It is much more likely that Putin knowingly instructed some of Steele's Russian sources to supply him with some credible-sounding disinformation that would later blow up in crooked Hillary's face (which it has). This is not to suggest that Putin favoured Trump over Clinton; only that his intention has always been to disrupt and embarrass the US electoral process.

In the case of Trump campaigners, they didn't approach the Russians for oppositional intel on Hillary; instead, the Russians approach them. In June 2016, Donald Trump Jr. and others met with a Russian lawyer and informant named Natalia Veselnitskaya who said she had damaging information about Hillary Clinton. But according to Trump Jr., "Her statements were vague, ambiguous and made no sense. No details or supporting information was provided or even offered." Probably sensing a devious Russian set-up, Trump Jr., without receiving any oppositional info on Hillary, wisely ended any further contact with Veselnitskaya. Who knows, if the Trump campaign had been as easily suckered-in as the Clinton campaign was, then they could have suffered the same embarrassing political fate—to Putin's great delight.

59. Hillary's efforts to hide the payments to Fusion GPS by routing them through her law firm, prompted the Campaign Legal Center (CLC) to file a complaint with

the Federal Election Commission (FEC) alleging the Democratic National Committee (DNC) and Hillary Clinton's 2016 campaign committee violated campaign finance law by failing to accurately disclose the purpose and recipient of payments for the dossier of research alleging connections between then-candidate Donald Trump and Russia. The CLC's complaint asserted that by effectively hiding these payments from public scrutiny the DNC and Clinton "undermined the vital public information role of campaign disclosures."

On October 24, The Washington Post revealed that the DNC and Hillary for America paid opposition research firm Fusion GPS to dig into Trump's Russia ties, but routed the money through the law firm Perkins Coie and described the purpose as "legal services" on their FEC reports rather than research. By law, campaign and party committees must disclose the reason money is spent and its recipient.

60. Republican Senator John McCain harboured a perpetually-burning hatred of Donald Trump ever since July 2015 when Trump declared: "He's not a war hero. He's a war hero because he was captured. I like people who weren't captured."

Several Vietnam war veterans have also denounced McCain, referring to him as the "Songbird" because he is alleged to have made 32 propaganda radio broadcasts when he was a POW (one damning "Tokyo Rose" style broadcast from 1969 is available on the internet from TruNews).

McCain also received special treatment from his North Vietnamese captors because his father, John S. McCain Jr., was an admiral in the US Pacific fleet at that time. As a deep-state swamp-rat senator, McCain managed to successfully cover up much of his "unheroic" past by having his POW records classified in perpetuity.

Though he claimed to be a Republican, McCain's foundation (McCain Institute) was partially funded by notorious, left-wing financier, George Soros)

CHAPTER 5

61. Please refer to the Saul Alinsky quotation from *Rules for Radicals: A Pragmatic Primer for Realistic Radicals* (1971) on page 15–16.
62. There are several ways of spelling "antichrist," including "Antichrist," "Anti-Christ" and "anti-Christ." This author's preferential usage is "Antichrist"; but in the case of direct quotations, the spelling used in the quotation has of course been retained.
63. The spiritual-scientific movement established by Rudolf Steiner in the early-twentieth century was called "anthroposophy" (Greek for "wisdom of man"). Steiner's own prodigious superphysical research has been recorded in 28 books, hundreds of articles and essays, and over 6000 lectures. For more detailed esoteric information on the profound differences between Lucifer and Satan, please refer to the series of lectures that Steiner gave in November 1919 and published in *The Influences of Lucifer and Ahriman: Man's Responsibility for the Earth* (1984); and this author's publication entitled *From Darkness to Light: Divine Love and the Transmutation of Evil* (2016).

OTHER BOOKS BY

RON MACFARLANE

THERE IS a puzzling and pervasive misconception in present-day thinking that the existence of God cannot be intellectually determined, and that mentally accepting the existence of God is strictly a matter of non-rational belief (faith).

As such, contemplating God's existence is erroneously regarded as the exclusive subject of faith-based or speculative ideologies (religion and philosophy) which have no proper place in natural scientific study.

The fact is, there are a number of very convincing intellectual arguments concerning the existence of God that have been around for hundreds of years. Indeed, the existence of God can be determined with compelling intellectual certainty—provided the thinker honestly wishes to do so. Moreover, recent advances and discoveries in science have not weakened previous intellectual arguments for God's existence, but instead have enormously strengthened and supported them.

Intellectually assenting to the existence of God is easily demonstrated to be a superlatively logical conclusion, not some vague irrational conceptualization. Remarkably, at the present time there are only two seriously-competing intellectual explanations of life: the existence of God (the "God-hypothesis") and the existence of infinite universes (the "multiverse theory"). The postulation of an infinite number of unobservable universes is clearly a desperate attempt by atheistic scientists to avoid the God-hypothesis as the most credible and logical intellectual explanation of life and the universe. Moreover, under intellectual scrutiny, the scientifically celebrated "evolutionary theory" is here demonstrated to be fatally-flawed (philosophically illogical) as a credible explanation of life.

In this particular discourse, five well-known intellectual arguments for God's existence will be thoroughly examined. In considering these arguments, every attempt has been made to include current contributions, advances and discoveries that have modernized the more traditional arguments. Prior to examining these particular arguments for God, the universal predilection to establish intellectual 'oneness'—"monism"—will be considered in detail as well as the recurring propensity to postulate the existence of one supreme being—"monotheism."

Once intellectual certainty of one Supreme Being is established, a number of divine attributes can be logically deduced as well. Eleven of these attributes will be determined and examined in greater detail.

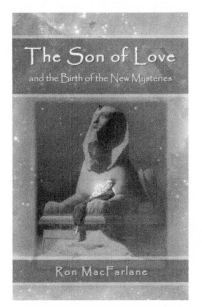

FOR COUNTLESS esoteric students today, the Mystery centres of ancient times have retained a powerful and fascinating allure. Moreover, there is often a wishful longing to revive and continue their secretive initiatory activity into modern times.

Unfortunately, this anachronistic longing is largely based on an illusionary misunderstanding of these Mysteries and the real reasons for their destined demise.

The primary reason for the disappearance of the ancient Mysteries is that they have been supplanted by the superior new mysteries—the mysteries of the Son. These new mysteries were initiated by Christ-Jesus himself. In order to better understand these Son-mysteries in a spiritually-scientific way, Rudolf Steiner (1861–1925) established the Anthroposophical Movement and Society.

Unfortunately, anthroposophy today has become unduly influenced by members and leaders who long to transform spiritual science into a modern-day Mystery institution. Moreover, contrary to his own words and intentions, Rudolf Steiner is even claimed to be the founder of some new "Michael-Mysteries."

By carefully establishing a correct esoteric understanding of the ancient pagan Mysteries, as well as a better appreciation of the new mysteries of the Son, this well-researched and readable discourse convincingly shows that all current and past attempts to revive the ancient pagan Mysteries regressively diverts human development backward to the seducer of mankind, Lucifer, rather than progressively forward to the saviour of mankind, Christ-Jesus.

Moreover, by additionally tracing the intriguing historical

development of esoteric Christianity (particularly the Knights of the Holy Grail and Rosicrucianism) alongside Freemasonry, the Knights Templar and Theosophy, this important and necessary study illuminates the correct esoteric position and true significance of anthroposophical spiritual science.

This book is available to order from Amazon.com

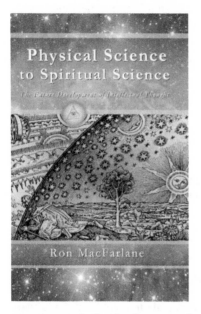

Physical Science to Spiritual Science

The Future Development of Intellectual Thought

Ron MacFarlane

THE PRIDE OF civilized mankind—intellectual thinking—is at a critical crossroads today. No doubt surprising to many, the cognitive capacity to consciously formulate abstract ideas in the mind, and then to manipulate them according to devised rules of logic in order to acquire new knowledge has only been humanly possible for about the last 3,000 years. Prior to intellectual (abstract) thinking, mental activity characteristically consisted of vivid pictorial images that arose spontaneously in the human mind from natural and supernatural stimuli.

The ability to think abstractly is the necessary foundation for mathematics, language and empirical science. The developmental history of intellectual thought, then, exactly parallels the developmental history of mathematics, language and science. Moreover, since abstract thinking inherently encourages the cognitive separation of subject (the thinker) and object (the perceived environment), the history of intellectual development also parallels the historical development of self-conscious (ego) awareness.

Over the last 3000 years, mankind in general has slowly perfected intellectual thinking; and thereby developed complex mathematics, sophisticated languages, comprehensively-detailed empirical sciences and pronounced ego-awareness. Unfortunately, all this intellectual activity over the many previous centuries has also exclusively strengthened human awareness of the physical, material world and substantially decreased awareness of the superphysical spiritual world.

195

That is why today, intellectual thinking is at a critical crossroads in further development. Thinking (intellectual or otherwise) is a superphysical activity—an activity within the soul. Empirical science is incorrect in postulating that physical brain tissue generates thought. The brain is simply the biological "sending and receiving" apparatus: sending sense-perceptions to the soul and receiving thought-conceptions from the soul. All this activity certainly generates chemical and electrical activity within the brain; but this activity is the effect, not the cause of thinking.

The danger to future intellectual thought is that increased acceptance of the erroneous scientific notion that thinking is simply brain-chemistry will increasingly deny and deaden true superphysical thinking. Future thinking runs the risk of becoming "a self-fulfilled prophecy"—the more people fervently believe that thought is simply brain-chemistry, the more thought will indeed become simply brain-chemistry. As a result, future human beings will be less responsible for generating their own thinking activity and more involuntarily controlled by their own brain chemistry. The artificial intelligence of machines won't become more human; but instead human beings will become more like robotic machines.

Presently, then, empirical science is leading intellectual thinking in a downward, materialistic direction. Correspondingly, however, true spiritual science (anthroposophy) is also actively engaged in leading intellectual thought back to its superphysical source in the soul. *Physical Science to Spiritual Science: the Future Development of Intellectual Thought* begins by examining the historical development of intellectual thinking and the corresponding rise of physical science. Once this has been discussed, practical and detailed information is presented on how spiritual science is leading intellectual thinking back to its true soul-source. It is intended that upon completion of this discourse, sincere and open-minded readers will themselves come to experience the exhilarating, superphysical nature of their own intellectual thought.

This book is available to order from Amazon.com

THE DIVINE TRINITY—the greatest of all Christian mysteries. How is it that the one God is a unity of three divine persons? Christ-Jesus first revealed this mystery to his disciples when on earth. Later, around the sixth century, the Trinitarian mystery was theologically clarified and outlined by the formulation of the Athanasian Creed. Conceptual understanding of the divine Trinity has changed very little in Western society since then. Similarly with the theological understanding of the Logos-Word, as mentioned in the Gospel of St. John. The traditional understanding, that has remained essentially unchallenged for centuries, is that the Logos-Word is synonymous with God the Son. As for creation, the best that mainstream Christianity has historically provided is an ancient, allegorical account contained in the Book of Genesis.

Out of the hidden well-springs of esoteric Christianity, and as the title indicates, *The Greater Mysteries of the Divine Trinity, the Logos-Word and Creation*, delves much more deeply into the profound mysteries of the Trinitarian God, the Logos-Word of St. John and the creation of the universe. The divine Trinity is here demonstrated to be the loving union of Heavenly Father, Holy Mother and Eternal Son. The Logos-Word is here evidenced to be the "Universal Man," the primordial cosmic creation of God the Son. Universal creation itself is here detailed to be the "one life becoming many"—the multiplication of the Logos-Word into countless individualized life-forms and beings.

The depth and breadth of original and thought-provoking information presented here will, no doubt, stimulate and excite those esoteric thinkers who are seriously seeking answers to the deeper mysteries of life, existence and the universe.

This book is available to order from Amazon.com

WHEN CHRIST-JESUS walked the earth over two thousand years ago, he established a two-fold division in his teaching that has continued to this day. To the general public, he simplified his teaching and presented it in pictorial, allegorical and figurative imagery in the form of stories, parables and lessons that could be imaginatively and intuitively understood.

To his inner circle of disciples (who were sufficiently prepared), however, he taught intellectual concepts, clear ideas and logical reasoning that could be understood on a much deeper and wider level of comprehension. As biblically explained:

> Then the disciples came and said to him, "Why do you speak to them [the general public] in parables?" And he answered them, "To you it has been given to know the secrets of the kingdom of heaven, but to them it has not been given ... This is why I speak to them in parables, because seeing they do not see, and hearing they do not hear, nor do they understand." (Matt 13:10, 13)

Moreover, in union with the divine, Our Saviour was able to reveal sacred knowledge that had never been previously presented in the entire history of mankind: "I will explain mysteries hidden since the creation of the world" (Matt 13:35). This sacred and revealed knowledge has been termed "Christ-mysteries" or "mysteries of the Son."

After his glorious resurrection and ascension, Christ-Jesus

institutionalized his two-fold mystery-teachings through St. Peter and St. John (the evangelist, not the apostle). Through St. Peter, Our Saviour instituted a universal Christian *religion* and *theology* to preserve, promote and convey the more basic and simplified mystery-teachings that are intended for the general public. Through St. John, Christ-Jesus instituted a universal Christian *philosophy* and *theosophy* to preserve, promote and convey the more comprehensive and complex mystery-teachings that are intended for the more advanced disciples (Christian initiates). In esoteric terminology, the institutionalized teachings through St. Peter are known as the "lesser mysteries of exoteric Christianity." The institutionalized teachings through St. John are known as the "greater mysteries of esoteric Christianity."

While both mystery-teaching approaches are equally sacred, profound and intended to complement each other, corrupt and intolerant authorities within the universal institution (Church) of St. Peter, for many centuries, persecuted and attacked any public expressions of esoteric Christianity. Consequently, genuine historical forms of esoteric Christianity, such as the Knights of the Holy Grail and the Fraternity of the Rose-Cross, were forced to be secretive and publically-hidden during the past two thousand years.

Thankfully today, the social, political and intellectual climate has progressed to the point where the greater mystery-teachings of esoteric Christianity can begin to be publically revealed for the first time. This modern-day outpouring really began with the twentieth-century establishment of anthroposophy by Rudolf Steiner (1861–1925). The information and approach presented in *The Star of Higher Knowledge: The Five Guiding Mysteries of Esoteric Christianity* is intended to augment and continue the mystery-teachings of Christ-Jesus as safeguarded by the Rosicrucian Fraternity and publicized through anthroposophy.

Consequently, this particular discourse delves much more deeply and comprehensively into the cosmos-changing salvational achievement of Christ-Jesus: the historical and cosmic preparations; as well as his birth, life, death, resurrection and ascension. While much of this mystery information may be unfamiliar, unknown and unexpected to mainstream (exoteric) Christianity, it in no way is meant to criticize, denigrate or displace the profound teachings of the universal Church; but rather, to complement, to enhance and to enlarge—for the betterment of true Christianity and, thereby, the betterment of all mankind.

This book is available to order from Amazon.com

Also check out the authour's website:

www.heartofshambhala.com

A Site Dedicated to True Esoteric Christianity

Contemporary Christianity, the world religion established by the God-Man, Christ-Jesus, and founded on the revelatory-principle that "God is love," is hardly the shining example of ideological unity and universal brotherhood that it was intended to be. There are approximately 41,000 different Christian denominations in the world today, many of which are fervently hostile to each other.

Atheistic and anti-Christian polemicists have concluded that there is something inherently wrong with Christianity itself and, in consequence, it is doomed to failure and eventual extinction.

Discerning Christian advocates, however, know that any apparent failure to realize the high ideals of Christianity is not due to the profound teachings and the illustrious life-example of Christ-Jesus, but instead to the limitations of wounded human nature. Corrupt, power-hungry, destructive and evil-minded human beings have twisted, distorted and fragmented true Christianity for the past two thousand years, and continue to do so today.

Moreover, on a much deeper spiritual level, since Christianity is indeed a divinely-initiated endeavor to help restore "fallen" humanity, powerful and demonic beings have attempted to destroy nascent Christianity from its very inception. But thankfully, according to Christ-Jesus himself, "the powers of hell will not prevail against it [Christianity]" (Matt 16:18).

Sadly contributing to the injurious fragmentation of Christianity—the "religion of divine love"—is the sectarian hostility between certain proponents of anthroposophy and select members of the Catholic Church. In both cases, this is largely due to ignorance; that is, an almost complete lack of understanding about the true significance and mission of the other—anthroposophical critics know almost nothing of Catholicism, and Catholic critics know almost nothing about anthroposophy.

The wonderful reconciliatory fact is that anthroposophy and Catholicism are not conflicting polar opposites, but are instead like two sides of the same golden coin—different, but complementary. Instead of only one side or the other being the only true approach to Christ-Jesus, both are uniquely necessary and both positively contribute to the complete truth of Christianity.

Since this author is happily and harmoniously both an anthroposophist and a Catholic, *The Greater and Lesser Mysteries of Christianity: The Complementary Paths of Anthroposophy and Catholicism* earnestly seeks to correct the misinformation and lack of understanding that each partisan critic has for the other. As in almost every significant dispute, increased knowledge and familiarity about each other will in time bring both sides closer together for mutual growth and benefit.

This book is available to order from Amazon.com

IN THE LIGHT of spiritual science, never before in the history of the world has there been such an assailment of supernatural evil upon humanity as extensive and intense as there exists at the present time. Subconsciously pouring into the human soul are the seductive whisperings of Luciferic beings and fallen angels; the perceptual distortions of Ahrimanic (Satanic) beings; the lurid, egocentric promptings of corrupt spirits of personality (asuras); and the violent inducements of blood-lust rising up from the subterranean "beast of Revelation" (Sorath the sun-demon).

The tragic and bitter irony of all this, however, is that because of today's pervasive, atheistic and secular culture and the materialistic worldview of natural science, individual human beings are correspondingly the most oblivious to supernatural evil than they have ever been at any other time in world history.

To be sure, people today are certainly aware of the *effects* of supernatural evil—extensive and increased natural disasters; horrific instances of mass genocide; the prolific use of torture and brutality by government agencies; individual acts of sudden cruelty and murder; pathological selfishness throughout the world's business and financial markets; strange, globally-infectious viral contagions; the devaluation of human life through abortion and euthanasia; and a world-wide pandemic of dehumanizing drug addiction. What most people today fail to realize is that the invisible fomenting agents—the *causes*—of all these life-threatening, destructive physical events and pathologies are ultimately rooted in the impulses of supernatural evil.

To be sure, mankind would have completely and totally succumbed to this tsunami of supernatural evil if it weren't for the protective and opposing intervention of powerful, benevolent celestial beings, such as St. Michael the Archai, Yahweh-Elohim (the spirit of the moon), and the Solar-Christos (aka: "Christ"—the regent of the sun).

More than ever, it is crucially important in today's world to understand the nature of evil, and to become more aware and cognizant of the various perpetrators of supernatural evil. Thereby, conscious cooperation with the compassionate protectors and guardians of mankind can be increased and strengthened, so that supernatural evil is better resisted and eventually overcome.

To this end, *From Darkness to Light: Divine Love and the Transmutation of Evil* delves deeply into the thorny questions of "What exactly is evil?"; together with "How and when did evil begin?"; as well as "Why does God allow evil to exist?" Once the nature, genesis and purpose of evil is better understood, then various influential superphysical perpetrators of supernatural evil will be examined in closer detail. Correspondingly, the superphysical proponents of cosmic holiness will be identified and better understood as well.

Wherever possible, the spiritual-scientific research of anthroposophy—an independent offshoot of the Rosicrucian Fraternity, and the modern-day expression of esoteric Christianity that was established by Rudolf Steiner (1861–1925)—will be included and referenced. Following this profoundly-esoteric background, the destined human struggle with continuing and obdurate evil—far into the future development of the earth—will also be mentally envisioned and supersensibly examined.

It is sincerely intended that upon completion of the entire written discourse, concerned individuals will be better armed and shielded in order to become actively engaged on the side of holiness and spiritual light in the prolonged cosmic battle against evil and material darkness.

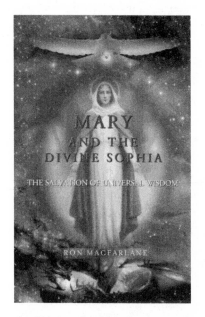

NO DOUBT, anyone interested in Christian esotericism will have noticed that there is a widespread modern-day revival of interest in the ancient gnostic concept of "Sophia" amongst a strange diversity of groups: wiccans, neo-pagans, New Agers, neo-gnostics, Catholic mystics, Orthodox Christians, radical feminists and anthropos-ophists. Adding to this ideological mélange is the exotic variety of Sophia designations and conceptions: the Divine Sophia, the heavenly-sophia, the earthly-sophia, Hagia Sophia, the goddess Sophia, the Aeon Sophia, the Virgin Sophia, Sophia-Achamoth, Pistis Sophia, Isis-Sophia, Jesus Sophia, theo-sophia, philo-sophia and anthropo-sophia.

Not surprisingly, then, this cacophony of Sophias is very often contradictory, confusing, distorted, invented, erroneous, and (sadly) rarely enlightening. It is not difficult to detect that "esoteric entrepreneurs" have seized this current "thirst for Sophia" to offer up a potpourri of books, courses, conferences, workshops, lessons, websites, video clips, internet articles—even worship services—to inundate, titillate and financially captivate any novice Sophia seeker.

So, what is a sincere Christian esotericist to make of this fervent Sophia phenomenon: "Is it a positive and healthy spiritual development, or is it a regressive and outmoded religious diversion?" This particular discourse—*Mary and the Divine Sophia*—delves deeply and genuinely into this important question in order to establish spiritual fact from unspiritual fiction.

In order to adequately answer this question, however, profound esoteric investigation into the Trinitarian nature of God, as well as the universal being of the Logos-Word, together with the fundamental underlying principles of the created cosmos will need to be detailed and discussed. Some of this previously-guarded esoteric information may be quite new and unfamiliar to many readers; but every effort has been made to present it in clear, understandable concepts.

Furthermore, since the mother of Jesus is very often intimately associated or connected to historical and present-day conceptions of Sophia, a comprehensive study will also be undertaken regarding Mary and her special relationship to the Divine Sophia; relying heavily on the spiritual-scientific research of Austrian philosopher and esotericist, Rudolf Steiner (1861–1925). Once again, a great deal of this information will be startlingly new to those unfamiliar with anthroposophy; but, as before, great care has been taken to present this possibly-unfamiliar information in a comprehensible, intellectually-accessible way.

It is sincerely intended that this discourse will provide the earnest esotericist with reliable, trustworthy and objective spiritual knowledge in order to confidently know and understand the mystery-truth of the heavenly-sophia; and thereby extricate her from the distortions and falsifications of Lucifer and Ahriman.

This book is available to order from Amazon.com

SINCE THE DAWN of mankind, human beings have unquestioningly accepted the self-evident biological truth that there are only two distinct sexes—male and female. Furthermore, this truth was understood to be divinely established, as indicated in the ancient Hebrew writings of Moses: "So God created man in his own image ... male and female he created them. And God blessed them" (Gen 1:27, 28).

Similarly with the concomitant truth that there are only two distinct genders—masculine and feminine. Moreover, in ancient times the dual genders were seen as fundamental and complementary universal principles that infused and fashioned everything in the created cosmos. One familiar expression of this ancient metaphysical belief is the Chinese Taoist principles of yin and yang.

Throughout history, stable and productive family units, tribal groupings, social communities, and even vast empires were globally established on the exigent foundational truths of sexuality and gender—that is—until very recently.

Beginning in the mid-1950s, what had been perennially and universally accepted regarding sex and gender began to be academically questioned and challenged. This ideological heterodoxy quickly accelerated in the 1960s with the inception and radical cultural impact of the sexual revolution and the feminist movement. Increased and well-organized gay and lesbian activism in the 1970s also did much to publicly reject the traditional dichotomies of male–female and masculine–feminine in order to

209

promote a novel range of non-normative sexualities and exotic gender categories.

By the early 2000s, sociological theorists, academic institutions, media organizations, civil rights groups, medical associations, political parties, national governments and international agencies were all becoming involved in a cultural drive to "mainstream" this radically-new and socially-transformative gender ideology.

But to a large percentage of today's citizens throughout Western society, this cultural revolution of gender ideology has been unexpectedly and uninvitedly infiltrating their established lives and communities with a discordant cacophony of bizarre sexual and gender ideas, terms and expressions; such as: gender identity, gender expression, gender roles, gender socialization, gender fluidity, gender ambiguity (ambigender), third gender (trigender), non-binary gender, non-gender, gender neutral, agender, gender dysphoria, gender perspective, genderqueer, biological gender, hormonal gender, gonadic gender, cisgender, pangender, transgender, sexual orientation, bisexual, transsexual, intersexual, omnisexual, asexual, androgynous and two-spirit.

While even to casual observation, it is evident that this contemporary sexual revolution is causing fierce political and social upheaval, what can be perplexing to a deeper spiritual analysis are questions such as: "What exactly are sexuality and gender; and are they synonymous or different? What is causing the current sexual revolution? Why is it occurring at this particular time in world history? Is this sexual revolution progressive or regressive; beneficial or harmful? Are there spiritual forces and beings involved in this upheaval; and are they godly or evil?"

Though these questions can certainly be spiritually addressed by traditional Western theology, a much deeper, meaningful, lasting and comprehensive understanding can only be provided by the superphysical research and hidden wisdom of esoteric science.

This particular discourse, then—*Gender and Sexuality in Light of Esoteric Science*—heavily relies on ancient Yogic teachings, age-old Egyptian Hermetic philosophy, hidden Rosicrucian wisdom and the anthroposophical research of clairvoyant investigator, Rudolf Steiner (1861–1925) to profoundly and penetratingly address these important questions.

Esoteric science will convincingly explain why there are, in reality, only two sexes—male and female; and only two genders—masculine and feminine. Anything else is an unreal and delusional abstraction, hypothesis or conjecture.

In order to rationally embrace the binary truth of gender—masculine and feminine—it will be necessary to first understand the Trinitarian nature of God, and then perceive how the divine nature is faithfully reflected throughout the created universe, including human existence. After which, in order to similarly embrace the binary truth of human sexuality—male and female—it will be necessary to clairvoyantly trace the history and development of mankind on earth, back to far-distant primordial ages.

It will be shown that throughout human existence on earth, powerful supernatural beings and forces—both beneficial and inimical—have been intimately and significantly involved in the evolution and development of human sexuality. Moreover, despite the appalling lack of contemporary human awareness, this supernatural involvement has continued into the present day.

The much-celebrated "freedoms" brought about by the sexual revolution will be seen and understood to be an inimical supernatural assault on reason, reality, nature and progressive human evolution, particularly by Luciferic and Ahrimanic beings and forces.[2] The current state of sexual and gender confusion, therefore, is not regarded as a positive development by esoteric science; but rather a seriously-harmful and seductive delusionary entrapment that must be challenged, arrested and positively corrected.

This book is available to order from Amazon.com

ABOUT THE AUTHOR

Ron is a 68 year-old, middle-class Canadian guy who is happily
retired from a professional career as a high school art teacher;
and who currently lives in Mission BC, Canada,
together with his loving wife Anne Marie,
close to their four adult daughters
and three wonderful grandchildren.
Having more free time in retirement,
Ron decided to form his own publishing company
Greater Mysteries Publications
and author a series of books
focusing primarily on esoteric Christianity.
All are available from Amazon.com.

Made in the USA
Monee, IL
22 March 2021